Alban Knecht
Social Work in the Changing Welfare State

Book Series of the Social Pedagogy Section of ÖFEB (Austrian Association of Research and Development in Education)

edited by
Sara Blumenthal, Alpen-Adria-Universität Klagenfurt
Stephan Sting, Alpen-Adria-Universität Klagenfurt
Karin Lauermann, Bundesinstitut für Sozialpädagogik Baden
Eberhard Raithelhuber, Bertha von Suttner Privatuniversität St. Pölten

Volume 15

Alban Knecht

Social Work in the Changing Welfare State

A Policy Analysis of Active Labour Market Policies for Disadvantaged Youth in Austria

Verlag Barbara Budrich
Opladen • Berlin • Toronto 2024

© 2024 This work is licensed under the Creative Commons Attribution 4.0 (CC-BY 4.0). It permits use, duplication, adaptation, distribution and reproduction in any medium or format, as long as you give appropriate credit to the original author(s) and the source, provide a link to the Creative Commons license and indicate if changes were made. To view a copy of this license, visit https://creativecommons.org/licenses/by/4.0/

The author acknowledges the financial support by the University of Klagenfurt.

The use of third party material in this book does not indicate that it is also subject to the Creative Commons licence mentioned. If the material used is not subject to the aforementioned Creative Commons licence and the action in question is not permitted by law, the consent of the respective rights holder must be obtained for further use. Trademarks, company names, generally descriptive terms etc. used in this work may not be used freely. The rights of the respective rights holder must be observed and use is subject to the rules of trademark law, even without separate reference.
This book is available as a free download from www.budrich.eu (https://doi.org/10.3224/84743053).

© 2024 by Verlag Barbara Budrich GmbH, Opladen, Berlin & Toronto
www.budrich.eu

      ISBN   978-3-8474-3053-7 (Paperback)
      eISBN 978-3-8474-1985-3 (PDF)
      DOI   10.3224/84743053

Verlag Barbara Budrich GmbH
Stauffenbergstr. 7. D-51379 Leverkusen Opladen, Germany
86 Delma Drive. Toronto, ON M8W 4P6 Canada
www.budrich.eu

A CIP catalogue record for this book is available from Die Deutsche Nationalbibliothek (The German National Library) (https://portal.dnb.de)

Carbon compensated production.

Cover design by Bettina Lehfeldt, Kleinmachnow – www.lehfeldtgraphic.de
Editing by Julia Stauber
English Proof-Reading by Katharina Rodgers

Acknowledgements

Which goals are pursued within the framework of social policy, which measures are implemented? How is social work influenced by social policy? How independent is social work in the implementation of its tasks? Is it largely determined by social policy?

This work explores these questions by analysing labour market policy measures for young people in Austria. It merges the thematic research and publications I have undertaken over the last ten years (since the publication of my dissertation) and further develops various themes towards more general questions of social pedagogy and social policy. The research is based on interviews with experts, professionals, and young people, all of whom I would like to thank for their efforts and information.

My special thanks go to Fabian Kessl and Stephan Sting, who accompanied and supported the habilitation process, as well as to Birgit Bütow, who also reviewed this work. I would like to thank the co-authors of some of the essays relevant to this work, Roland Atzmüller, Franz-Christian Schubert, Luca Preite and, Michael Bodenstein for their pleasant and fruitful collaboration, as well as my colleagues at the Department of Social Pedagogy and Inclusion Research in Klagenfurt, Sara Blumenthal, Ernst Kočnik, Rahel More, Marion Sigot and Stephan Sting for the important collegial exchange and the repeated discussions on earlier versions of this work. The freedom and structure of my tax-funded post-doctoral position at the University of Klagenfurt were another factor that made the completion of this publication possible.

I would also like to thank the participants of the Dissertation and Habilitation Colloquiums in Wuppertal, Germany, organised by Fabian Kessl, for the valuable exchange and discussions. Last but not least, I would like to thank the members of the Habilitation Committee as well as my supporters Daniela Blank, Philipp Catterfeld, Karoline Feyertag, Ulrich Hofmeister, Dagmar Knecht, Alexa Krebs, Michi Matthes, Andrea Messerschmid, Jessica Richter, Katharina Rodgers, Peter Schlögl and Julia Stauber.

Table of contents

List of tables and figures 9

1   Youth employment promotion in the changing welfare state.........11
1.1 Challenges at the transition from school to vocational training 11
1.2 Changes in the welfare state and the increasing socio-political importance of education 13
1.3 Changes in the framework conditions of social work 15
1.4 Structure of the work 18

2   The Resource Theory perspective as a theoretical framework 21
2.1 Resource Theory (IMTM) at a glance 21
2.2 Resource Theory (IMTM) as a multidimensional theory of inequality 22
2.3 Resource Theory (IMTM) as a socio-political theory 26
2.4 Resource Theory (IMTM) in social work 29
2.5 Understanding the mechanisms of resource distribution by analysing discourses and institutions – the role of political guiding principles and mission statements 32

3   Changing discourses on labour market policies for youth and youth employment promotion 43
3.1 Notes on design and method 43
3.2 Public discourses on youth unemployment and labour market policies for youth 44
3.3 The discourses of experts and professionals and their political significance 49
3.4 Discourses of professionals working in the field and subjectification by young people 53
3.5 Results of the discourse analysis 55

4   Institutional changes of youth employment support in the government coalitions in Austria (2000–2020) 57
4.1 ÖVP-FPÖ-Coalition I (2000–2007): The expansion of the company-oriented apprenticeship promotion 58
4.2 SPÖ-ÖVP-Coalition (2007–2017): From the training guarantee to compulsory training 60

4.3 ÖVP-FPÖ-Coalition II (2017–2019): The activation of Austrian youths and the blocking of young asylum-seekers 65

5 Results and conclusions: On the governance of the welfare state .. 71
5.1 Results of discourse analysis and institutional analysis 71
5.2 Social inequalities and new divisions – issues of social justice 75
5.3 Right-wing populist/extreme right social policy as a hierarchising and exclusionary policy of prevention 77
5.4 Thinking the welfare state "from below" 81

6 Impact of socio-political change on social work and on young people 83
6.1 Changing social pedagogy of transition through social investment labour market policy 83
6.2 The quasi-pedagogy of the market and right-wing populist/extreme-right exclusionary politics 86
6.3 Discrimination and lack of recognition as problems of young people and as an issue of social work 88
6.4 Lack of opportunities for participation and the possibility of vocational political training 91

7 Conclusion and outlook 95

8 Tabels 100

9 References 109

10 Index 137

List of tables and figures

List of tables

Table 1: Ratios of educational attainment and early school leavers by gender 100
Table 2: Unemployment rates by age and apprenticeship supply in Austria.. 102
Table 3: Promotion/Subsidies for the youth active labour market policies (in € million)... 104
Table 4: Number of apprentices and participants in measures................... 106

List of figures

Figure 1: Multi-level model of Resource Theory (IMTM) 27
Figure 2: Overview of guiding principles 34

1 Youth employment promotion in the changing welfare state

1.1 Challenges at the transition from school to vocational training

Adolescence is considered a phase of transition from childhood to adulthood and an important developmental phase that is particularly vulnerable. While the idea of adolescence is associated with trying out different ways of living and acting, at the same time it represents a phase in which educational processes play a central role and educational decisions set the course for the future (Reinders 2016; Reinders/Wild 2003). The demands of moving through the formal education system and achieving formal qualifications can bring a sense of achievement and self-efficacy, but can also create pressure and uncertainty. Decisions in favour of a particular school or training pathway have a far-reaching influence on the rest of their lives. While young people attending higher education are more challenged by formal learning requirements, young people starting an apprenticeship in the Austrian dual system of vocational education and training are expected to integrate quickly into the world of work (Sting/Knecht 2022). Those young people who are perceived to have "problems" in the transition from school to training and work are particularly burdened and challenged.

In the context of international comparisons, the dual VET system common in German-speaking countries is said to have a high integrative power as it enables a majority of young people who do not want to or are unable to pursue school or academic education to obtain qualifications (cf. AMS Austria 2016: 18; Knecht/Atzmüller 2017: 239). However, the training system itself is under pressure, especially due to an ever-decreasing supply of apprenticeship places, and is undergoing strong changes (Knecht/Atzmüller 2019: 216). In Austria, for example, the number of apprenticeships has decreased from 124,000 in 2000 to 101,700 in the pre-Corona year 2019.[1] In the same period, the number

---

[1] The realized number of apprenticeships results from the supply of and demand for apprenticeship places. The demand for apprenticeship places depends on the number of young people who aspire to an apprenticeship, i.e. on educational aspirations, as well as on the strength of the cohort. Looking at the development of the cohort of 15-year-olds in Austria, their number declined from almost 100,000 to 86,000 between 2008 and 2018. A constant number of about 87,000 per year is expected until 2025 (Dornmayr/Nowak 2019: 50). If the demand for apprenticeships is higher than the supply, this makes it difficult for young people to find an apprenticeship/training place.

of companies providing training places has fallen from 39,300 to 27,800 (Dornmayr/Löffler 2020: 67). The situation in Austria with an unemployment rate of 15- to 19-year-olds in 2019 of 10.9% is nevertheless less problematic in a European comparison, where unemployment rates of young people sometimes exceed 40–50%. The unemployment rates of 20- to 24-year-olds (see Table 1) show that a large part of young adults succeed in integrating into the labour market, but that many young adults are also affected by unemployment and precariousness.

Despite great efforts and a high financial outlay, the youth unemployment rate does not decrease (Tab. 1). Especially during crises, such as the real estate and economic crisis in 2002, the banking and financial crisis in 2008f. and the Corona crisis in 2020/2021, it rises again and again; companies offer fewer apprenticeships. Although it is evident that economic cycles play an important role in (youth) unemployment, in public discourse it is primarily interpreted as a problem of young people with deficits and a lack of training maturity. The frequently discussed thesis that young people are increasingly deficient and that there are more problems filling apprenticeship positions with suitable applicants is, however, paradoxical against the background of a permanently increasing formal education level of youths and young adults and a long-term trend towards ever higher school-leaving qualifications. For example, the rates of early school leavers fell from 10.2% to 7.8% between 2010 and 2019 in Austria (see Tab. 1 and Statistics Austria 2021a). At the same time, there has been and continues to be a strong trend towards higher education, e.g. at universities, universities of applied sciences and colleges, leading to a permanent increase in upper secondary and tertiary level qualifications (see Tab. 2). The proportion of young people in a cohort who start an apprenticeship has remained relatively constant; in Austria it is around 40% (Dornmayr/Nowak 2019: 23).

Despite the high educational aspirations, the picture of a less interested and less educated youth is often drawn or it is assumed that at least the less educated would increasingly show deficits[2], thus causing unemployment. In the discussion, however, it is neither discussed that the trend of increasing educational levels of young adults during the last years has not led to a decrease in unemployment figures, nor that high rates of higher educational qualifications lead to their devaluation and to an "intensification of the competition on the labour market" (Fasching 2019: 854)[3] go hand in hand with this.

2 For example, in an interview with the SocIEtY project, a senior administrator pointed out us that "genetically, the distribution tends to go down, so to speak – I don't want to be judgmental now ..." (quote from the SocIEtY project; Atzmüller/Knecht 2017b: 123), because better students would increasingly choose higher educational careers and school leavers who would have become unskilled workers under earlier conditions would now aspire to an apprenticeship. This interpretation is based on an undynamic notion of competence acquisition.
3 All German-language citations are translated by A.K.

The combination of the fact that the apprenticeship market tends to be unbalanced, a changing understanding of social policy as well as the succession of different political coalitions, leads to both a continuing commitment of the government ("governance") in the area of employment support for disadvantaged young people in Austria – especially when crises occur (Atzmüller/Décieux/Knecht 2019), as well as ongoing (social) policy interventions and permanent changes.

1.2 Changes in the welfare state and the increasing socio-political importance of education

In the 1970s and 1980s, the welfare state was still thought of as an institution that established legitimacy by putting the forces of capitalism in check and limiting its negative excesses (e. g. Esping-Andersen 1990). In the post-war period, Thomas H. Marshall had even modelled the development of citizenship in the (welfare) state as a sequence of steps towards civil, political and social rights (Marshall/Bottomore 1992). Kaufmann (2005) describes in this sense the essence of the welfare state as interventions that improve the legal situation, the monetary situation, the education and the socio-ecological environment of the citizens.

Since the 1990s at the latest, the hitherto prevailing view of the functioning of the welfare state has been questioned and challenged in practically all European countries within the framework of neoliberal arguments. In the Fordist-Keynesian model of the post-war period, the welfare state also had the task of enabling mass consumption in order to moderate the contradiction between the "interests of capital" – i.e. of investors and entrepreneurs – and the interests of dependent workers, as well as the task of bridging demand shortfalls through state spending (investment and social spending) in order to counteract the deepening of crises (Böhnisch et al. 2012). Within the framework of neoliberal projects, however, imperfect markets and the alleged lack of flexibility of the "labour factor" were placed in the foreground; accordingly, the legal protection of labour relations was weakened, transfer payments were cut and thus labour was recommodified (Atzmüller/Décieux/Knecht 2019: 111). In many countries, the transformation of the welfare state[4] from the 1990s onwards has hardly led to the expected dismantling of welfare state services, but rather to their being restructured. As far as social and educational policies for children and youth are concerned, the strategies of making labour markets more flexible also provided future employees with new ways of adapting, recomposing and

---

[4] See for an overview of the transformation e.g. Götsch/Kessl 2017; Betzelt/Fehmel 2022; Kessl 2013; Nullmeier/Rüb 1993.

transforming labour assets (ibid.). Within this framework, education was increasingly considered as a part of social policy (Opielka 2005a; Kohlrausch 2014). In the academic context, this was justified, among other things, by the special role of education in the process of reproducing social inequality (e. g. Fischer 2020: 373). Thus, the expansion of day care centres, all-day schools and an expanded management of transition were associated with hopes of equalising wages and incomes (Esping-Andersen et al. 2002; Esping-Andersen 2003).

As a theoretical model of the welfare state, the social investment approach was then frequently cited – and was partly positioned as a counter-model to neoliberalism (Giddens 2000; critical: Atzmüller/Knecht 2017a). In this approach, profitable investments in citizens, especially in the field of education, serve as a new legitimisation of welfare state activity (Schroeder/Blair 1999). Educational opportunities are supposed to pave the way for a self-reliant life that is economically secured through the utilisation of one's own educational resources. Day care centres, crèches and kindergartens were discovered to be educational institutions which, by caring for children, at the same time provide a better utilisation of parental educational resources (Esping-Andersen 2002). However, in this context, the resource education is primarily thought of as human capital, which primarily serves to improve the skills that are in demand on the labour market and to increase employability (Knecht/Atzmüller 2017: 245).

These shifts were accompanied by changes in public discourses: Individuals' lifestyles were now ascribed increased importance. The responsibility for one's educational and professional career is placed in one's own hands, and failure in the educational and professional markets is more strongly seen as individualised and be interpreted as "not wanting" rather than "not being abto to", which is sanctioned accordingly (Atzmüller/Décieux/Knecht 2019: 112f.) without taking barriers and unfavourable framework conditions into account. In this context, the welfare state becomes more disciplinary and punitive (see below). The question of who deserves or does not deserve what kind of help has been posed in a new way, and the discourses that distinguish between deserving and undeserving recipients of benefits, which were thought to have been overcome, have been revived (e.g. Knecht 2010: 162f.).

In Austria, too, social policy has developed towards a social-investment and activating social state, even if the term social investment rarely appears in public discourse (cf. Buxbaum 2014) and most developments were implemented with a time lag compared to other European countries.[5] For example,

---

5 Compared to the introduction of Hartz IV, Austria seems to confirm the bon mot attributed to Karl Kraus: "When the world ends, I'll go to Vienna. There everything happens ten years later." With regard to other topics, however, there are also other chronological sequences, e.g. with regard to the development of private

a reform of the minimum income system in Austria similar to the Hartz-IV reform was not implemented until 2018.[6]

In the context of establishing a social investment policy, the importance of promoting the employment of disadvantaged young people has also increased. Vocational training (and in the German-speaking countries particularly: apprenticeships) promises to increase the employability of youths and young adults. On the one hand, employment support is a future-oriented part of labour market policy, and on the other hand it is an area of pedagogical intervention, which is highlighted by the term *Vocational Youth Welfare* ("Jugendberufshilfe"), which is commonly used in Germany (Enggruber/Fehlau 2018). In Austria, the introduction of a training guarantee in 2008 and a training obligation in 2018 (see below, chapter 4.2) points to the growing educational and socio-political importance of this field, but also to new values and standardisations that are part of the transformation of social work taking place in Austria.[7]

1.3 Changes in the framework conditions of social work

With the above-mentioned change in the welfare state, some framework conditions and objectives of social work as well as social work itself have changed, which critical positions assume to be due to the economisation associated with the spread of New Public Management (Eichinger 2009: 58f; Leibetseder 2016: 56) and the implementation of the activation paradigm.

Usually, the introduction of market-based or market-like control mechanisms in the area of social services are understood as part of the economisation of the welfare sector (Hammerschmidt 2014). One of the resulting changes was the introduction of the new public management model which has reformed municipal administration with its features of decentralisation of specialist and resource responsibility, contracts and target agreements between politics and administration as well as between the administrative units, cost and performance accounting, and monitoring/controlling with output and outcome orientation (Kessl/Otto 2002: 446; Hammerschmidt 2014). Economisation and new public

---

bankruptcy, which was introduced earlier in Austria than in Germany, or the more far-reaching obligation in the area of kindergarten (Atzmüller/Décieux/Knecht 2019).

6   A merger of unemployment benefits and unemployment assistance (corresponding to the German unemployment assistance called 'Hartz IV') has not been realised (so far), although this was proposed by the last government of the coalition of ÖVP and FPÖ (2017–2019, see chapter 4.3). No work-first policy comparable to the one-euro jobs, which are a kind of forced labour has been established so far.

7   Bakic/Diebäcker/Hammer 2008; Diebäcker et al. 2009a; Diebäcker/Hammer 2009; Diebäcker et al. 2009b.

management form the basis of a way of thinking that focuses on economic categories and abstracts from or negates many (social) pedagogical, social work and psychological aspects. Performance agreements, for example, require institutions to achieve formal goals agreed upon in advance. This can be problematic for social work, if the effects consist of changes in people that only become visible in the long term and therefore cannot be presented as short-term goal achievement. In addition, on a very practical level, performance agreements and output monitoring, e.g. for staff, lead to short-term contracts in projects and higher economic pressure – which is on the one hand contrary to longer-term professionalisation and on the other hand problematic when the pressure is passed on to the clients. The neoliberal understanding of the economy (see below) and the "neo-social reprogramming of the social" (Kessl/Otto 2002) are in the background of economisation. This links the economisation to broader changes in the welfare state, such as a.) the orientation of education policy, social policy and societal policy towards the competitiveness of the economy, b.) the expectation that low social benefits generate motivation, c.) the moralisation of societal and financial success and failure, d.) the attribution of increased responsibility to citizens and clients, activation, and e.) increasing monitoring and punishment (Kessl 2018; Forster 2010; Büschken 2017; Hammerschmidt 2014).

The starting point for activation is a reinterpretation of the relationship between citizens and the state, a "shift of the causes of problems and a responsibility to deal with them to those affected [...] – as individual failure, lack of discipline, self-control or activity" (Lutz 2013: 26; see also Kessl/Otto 2002; Kessl 2013; Büschken 2017). Making those affected persons responsible for their situation ("responsibilisation") negates the significance of unfortunate coincidences, strokes of fate and the social barriers and framework conditions that reproduce social inequalities. Children and young people gradually grow from a state in which, due to their age, no responsibility for their situation is attributed to them, into a situation in which responsibility is attributed to them – without actually (always) having control over the course of their lives.

The increase of control/monitoring, disciplining and sanctioning as part of activation, plays a special role for social work. On the one hand, it must be noted that the exercise of control has always been present as one side of the coin of social work – alongside help as the other side (Lutz 2013) and has also been an ever-present theme of theorisation (s. a. Knecht/Preite 2022: 126) since the formulation of the *double mandate* (Böhnisch/Lösch 1973). On the other hand, help and control/monitoring have different meanings in different fields of action of social work. Open youth work, for example, often claims to be there for the young people in the context of emancipatory youth work (Hartwig 2000), to promote their independence and self-responsibility and to support them in "finding themselves" in identity processes (Knecht 2014: 222), whereas the youth education system fulfils a socialising and controlling/monitoring function. (Obviously, the control aspects are more prominent in areas focusing on job placement.)

Kessl (2013) shows that in the context of the double mandate, the two aspects of assistance and control are inextricably linked. A professional approach would take exactly this constellation into account: The "discovery" of the linkage of help and control as a basic challenge of social work at the beginning of the 1970s "marked the provisional end of the punitive programme in the social work/social education professional discussion" (Kessl 2013: 116). Punishment as an educational measure was also viewed increasingly critically until the 1980s (ibid.). Since the 1990s, however, a new willingness to control and to punish has been spreading – based on a new way of governing, especially among a newly discovered underclass (Wacquant 2009), which not only affects the framework conditions of social work (Kessl/Reutlinger/Ziegler 2007) but also the actions of social pedagogues/workers and the (social) pedagogical and social work procedures in the institutions (Kessl 2013). However, Kessl agrees with Lutz that there has been a change in the overall construction, in which the "conflict over help and control is now being replaced by the 'conflict over the legitimacy of the means, resulting in the question of how much coercion is allowed in help'" (ibid.: 118, as cited in Lutz 2010: 271), being replaced.

Lutz also points out a difference between support, in which help and control are inextricably interwoven, on the one hand, and social services, which are split into *help for the integrated* and *control for the excluded,* on the other hand (Lutz 2013: 25). In fact, within the framework of the activating labour market policy in Germany, which was advertised as "promote and challenge" (in German: "fordern und fördern"), there were and still are different action programmes designed to either "promote" or "challenge" – the latter having to be translated as "be sanctioned" (cf. Klevenow/Knecht 2013). Ultimately, this could mean – according to Lutz – for social work to distinguish interventions in the following way: "*a.)* voluntary offers for the active who are able and willing to face the demands [...]; *b.)* working with those who are considered to be able to be activated, with integration aids, pressure and disciplinary means to normalise them; *c.)* managing and controlling those who are not able to do so; and *d.)* discipling or excluding those who are labelled as 'dangerous'" (Lutz 2010: 206). Economisation, activation and disciplining thus represent different parts of the transformation of social work, which also results from a changed understanding of social policy. Referring to these connections, this paper examines the extent to which changes in the specific field of employment promotion for young people in Austria occur within the framework of changed social policy perspectives, which shall be explained in more detail in the following.

1.4 Structure of the work

Against the background of neoliberal and social-investment trends in social policy and of the changes in the field of social work, this paper brings together my findings of recent years to answer the question of how employment support for disadvantaged young people as part of social policy changed in Austria between 2000 and 2020 and what impact this change has had on the framework conditions of social educators, social workers and other professionals working in this field, as well as on young people.

The theoretical framework of this paper is the Resource Theory (Knecht 2010; Knecht 2012c, 2012b, 2012a, 2011; Knecht/Schubert 2012, 2020; Knecht et al. 2014; Schubert/Knecht 2015; Knecht 2016). As a social political theory, Resource Theory focuses on the question which social processes determine the broad spectrum of resources such as education, income, social resources, health, mental resources etc. that is allocated to individuals. The frequently discussed distributive function of social policy – and in this specific case the promotion of employment for young people – can thus be viewed comprehensively. The Resource Theory is presented in overview in chapter 3. Within the framework of this theory, on the one hand, discourses are considered which deal with the allocation (and, if applicable, the containment) of resources, legitimised them and constitute the basis for their (social) political distribution. On the other hand, state or state-organised institutions that carry out the allocation/distribution of resources are considered (see chapter 2.5).

The employment promotion of disadvantaged young people, which in Germany is also treated under the term "Vocational Youth Welfare" (in German: "Jugendberufshilfe"), represents a special area of youth policy and support for young people: Here, youth policy, general social policy and specific labour market policy as well as economic policy interests converge and have to be mediated. The question of how resources are allocated is therefore subject to a special constellation of influences that make analyses in this area particularly exciting.

From a methodological point of view, the empirical analyses in this manuscript represent interpretative policy analyses within the framework of policy field analyses (see below). They are based on various projects and investigations, namely

- the primarily Austria-related results of the EU-7 framework research project SocIEtY. Within the framework of a policy field analysis, a document analysis[8] and a content-analytical evaluation of 19 expert interviews were

---

8   Document analysis of official reports from ministries and administrative bodies, evaluation reports and descriptions of measures and programmes published by actors in the field of youth policy (Knecht/Kuchler/Atzmüller 2014: 495).

conducted (Knecht/Kuchler/Atzmüller 2014; Atzmüller/Knecht 2016a, 2017b; Acconcia et al. 2017; Atzmüller/Décieux/Knecht 2019),[9]
- an exploratory teaching research containing interviews with youth coaches as well as (group) interviews with young people (Knecht/Atzmüller 2019),[10]
- Analyses within the framework of a critical discourse analysis, on the minimum income and employment policy of the 2017–2019 government period (Atzmüller/Knecht/Bodenstein 2020),[11]
- a supplementary document analysis of National Council documents[12] and official reports on labour market policy for young people between the years 2000 and 2020 (see chapter 4).

The period under study from 2000 to 2020 was characterised on the one hand by the two "Black-Blue government periods" of the conservative Austrian People's Party ÖVP and the populist/extreme right Freedom Party of Austria FPÖ (supplementary: BZÖ) (2000–2007 and 2017–2019), and on the other hand by the "Red-Black government period" of the Austrian Social-Democratic Party SPÖ and the conservative Austrian People's Party ÖVP (2007–2017). While the promotion of employment for young people in the periods of the coalition of the conservative party ÖVP and the populist/extreme right party FPÖ (called "Black-Blue Coalition") revolved more around subsidising and promoting companies providing training, the beginning of the period of the coalition of the social democratic SPÖ and the conservative ÖVP was characterised by the rapid introduction of the training guarantee (2008) and eventually turned into a training duty.

---

9   Reports: Knecht/Kuchler/Atzmüller 2014, Reprint in: Haidinger et al. 2016; Haidinger/Knecht 2015. The SocIEtY project ("Social Innovation – Empowering the Young for the Common Good") was carried out under the EU's 7th Research Framework Programme (SSH.2012.2.1-1: Social innovation against inequalities, contract no.: 320136, duration: 2013–2015) and coordinated by Bielefeld University. The consortium consisted of 13 partner institutes in eleven countries.
10 See also AG Jugendforschung 2018. Data used only with student consent.
11 This analysis was based on extensive research on relevant policy documents (e.g. government programmes, legislative texts) as well as on the public and academic debates on the planned and implemented reforms. For the analysis of ideological articulations and images mobilised by the government, we collected all press statements of the coalition parties (ÖVP: N=48; FPÖ: N=49 out of a total of N=312) from APA-OTS (a website of the Austrian Press Agency that publishes press releases) between 1st of Jan. 2018 and 30th of April 2019 that dealt with the 'means-tested minimum income scheme' ("Bedarfsorientierte Mindestsicherung" = BMS).
12 In the Mediathek (= electronic archive) of the Austrian Parliament, named National Council, 59 documents (mainly drafts, resolutions, stenographic minutes) were identified in the section "Parlament aktiv"/"alle Verhandlungsgegenstände" with the keyword "Arbeitsmarkt" ("labour market") and the search term "Jugend" ("youth") and supplemented e.g. by parliamentary correspondence, press releases, and the like.

The third chapter is devoted to looking at changes in social policy discourses with a focus on youth employment promotion; the fourth chapter examines the institutional changes in this area. These two chapters correspond to the two points of analysis: discourse analysis and institutional analysis. In the fifth chapter, the results of the welfare state analyses are examined in greater depth. The sixth chapter looks at the changes in the framework conditions of social work and the consequences for young people. The seventh chapter summarises the results.

2 The Resource Theory perspective as a theoretical framework

2.1 Resource Theory (IMTM) at a glance

Resource Theory (IMTM), which is presented in the following, looks at the possibilities for individuals' action that result from the resources available to them. For this purpose, the approach considers resources such as income (money), education, health, psychological and social resources, etc. The resources available to individuals are not equal. Unequal resource endowments are associated with unequal opportunities for action and unequal social positions, which is why this *Resource Theory* can be used to describe social inequality in terms of the sociology of inequality (multidimensional). As a *sociological theory of inequality,* the *Resource Theory* presented contributes to explaining the emergence, maintenance (persistence) and reproduction of social inequality. However, it goes beyond theories of inequality and also represents *a socio-political theory*. As such, it focuses on how socio-political interventions affect the individual endowment with resources and on which "mechanisms" the distribution/allocation of resources is (socio)politically organised.

The *Resource Theory* presented here is interdisciplinary, multidimensional, transformational and multilevel in conception and is referred to in short form as *Resource Theory (IMTM)* (see below) to distinguish it from other approaches, such as theories on social justice or psychological resource theories. It was sketched in my dissertation thesis on "*Quality of Life. A Resource Theory and Power Analysis of the Welfare State"* (Knecht 2010), outlined in some smaller writings (Knecht/Buttner 2008; Buttner/Knecht 2009) and subsequently elaborated – in particular through joint editorship (Knecht/Schubert 2012; Schubert/Knecht 2012a, 2016) and authorship (Schubert/Knecht 2012b, 2015)- with Franz-Christian Schubert as well as with other colleagues (Knecht et al. 2014) and in several individual contributions (Knecht 2011, 2012a, 2012b, 2012c, 2016). In this context, *Resource Theory (IMTM)* was integrated into the context of social work – as well as poverty research (Knecht/Schenk 2023). Resource theory was conceived with reference to the discussion of resources in different disciplines. In overcoming a reduced economic concept of resources (cf. Schubert/Knecht 2012b; Hanesch 2012; Sen 1992, 1985; Dworkin 2011), it also draws on sociological theories, Amartya Sen's *capability approach,* as well as psychological and social work theories (see below and Knecht/Schubert 2020) and political theories (see below). In this respect, this Resource Theory is an *interdisciplinary theory* (even if it can be seen as a specific sociological theory of social inequality and social policy due to its explanatory potential and its functionality (see chapters 2.3 and 2.4)). Furthermore, it represents a *multidimensional theory*, since – like other approaches to poverty research[13] – it depicts social inequality (and poverty, if applicable) multidimensionally by including various resources. The different dimensions are not seen as independent of each other, but in their interaction, i.e. in the way resources are transformed into other kinds of resources (this is especially important for describing the persistence and reproduction of inequality). Resource theory is therefore also *transformation-related*. Last but not least, it looks at the emergence of individual resource endowments in the (socio-)political multi-level process. Therefore, the *Resource Theory* presented here is referred to as interdisciplinary, multidimensional, transformational and multilevel *Resource Theory* – or *Resource Theory (IMTM)* for short (Knecht/Schenk 2023). According to its functions, it can also be called the "resource theory of social inequality and social policy" and furthermore serve as an umbrella theory for social work. In the following, for the sake of simplicity, we will only refer to *Resource Theory,* as there is no danger of confusion with other resource approaches or theories. In chapter 2.2 *Resource Theory* is presented as a multidimensional theory of inequality. The chapters 2.3 and 2.4 focus on its usefulness as a socio-political theory and as a multidimensional inequality theory, respectively.

2.2 Resource Theory (IMTM) as a multidimensional theory of inequality

In general, resources are understood as means, conditions, characteristics or properties that serve to pursue goals, cope with requirements, carry out specific actions or complete a process in a goal-oriented manner (Knecht/Schubert 2020). Resources open up individual scope for action; therefore, the endowment with resources can be regarded as an indicator of the ability to act. My attempt to develop and elaborate a social science theory of resources that is grounded in both inequality theory and socio-politics aims to examine the resource endowment of actors multidimensionally at the individual level. These resources include income/money, education, social resources, health and psychological resources. Depending on the focus of the analysis, different resources can be in the foreground. For example, space and (the availability of)

---

13 In addition to the living-situational approach ("Lebenslagenansatz"), which is widespread in German-speaking countries but whose spectrum of dimensions used is not theoretically well-founded, a broad discussion on multidimensional poverty research has become established internationally, especially with regard to the multidimensional description of poverty (see e.g. Alkire et al. 2015).

time can also be understood as resources.[14] In the case of time as a resource, it is not only absolute durations that are important, e.g. of working hours, but also issues such as pace, plannability, synchronisation and time sovereignty (Jorck et al. 2019). Resources can be incorporated, attributed to a person (e.g. property) or located in the (wider) environment of a person (Knecht/Schubert 2020: 314). While the consideration of the former has a firm place in the sociology of social inequality, considerations of unequal health tend to be made in the context of a special social-epidemiological discourse (remote from politics); a discussion of an unequal endowment with psychologic/mental resources according to socially unequal positions in society hardly exists in the context of the sociology of inequality. Even in psychology the relevance of social inequality is often neglected.

In *Resource Theory (IMTM)*, on the other hand, the availability of psychological/mental resources is described with reference to psychological resource approaches as an essential factor for action (ebd; Schubert/Knecht 2020; Knecht 2016; Schubert 2016; Knecht/Schubert 2012; Schubert/Knecht 2012b; Schubert 2012). I refer to various psychological resource theories that have emerged since the 1970s. Foa and Foa, for example, looked at the exchange of resources, e.g. of couples, within the framework of *resource exchange theory* (Foa/Foa 1976; Törnblom/Kazemi 2012). Other early approaches addressing psychological/mental resources mostly dealt with coping with stress under psychological demands and thus also established links to psycho-social health concepts (Lazarus/Folkman 1984; cf. Schubert/Knecht 2015). Resilience theories (e.g. Werner 1977; cf. Schubert 2012) and the salutogenesis model (Antonovsky 1987) ask about resources as forms of coping. Thus Antonovsky (1987) considers the sense of coherence as a "hinge resource" for the ability to process stress and for the establishment or maintenance of mental and physical health. Hobfoll's theory of resource maintenance (Hobfoll 1988; 1989) examines the effect of stressful, stress-producing life situations on the resource situation of individuals. In his theory of resource conservation, he focuses on the perspective of the longer-term management of resources. Apart from addressing material resources, he refers to the individually different perception and cognitive processing of stress as well as to individual experiences of effectiveness. Together with his colleagues, he considers the possibility of preventing stress on a societal level, among other things through community-oriented coping, to be essential because the significance of the individual's resources always has to be seen in the socio-cultural context (Buchwald/Schwarzer/Hobfoll 2004; Hobfoll/Jackson 1991).

Resource Theory (IMTM) also draws on the concept of types of capital of Bourdieu (1992), who famously shows how individual actors use social capital and cultural/educational capital, in addition to financial capital, to protect or

---

14 See also Knecht/Schubert 2020. On the resource of time, see Klammer 2012 and Muckenhuber 2014.

secure their social status and privileges. Like resources, types of capital generate possibilities for action (cf. Meulemann 2004: 131f.). However, for an adequate development of a resource-theoretical approach, I consider it necessary to bring to the fore the potential for action bound up in the capitals or in the resources (Knecht/Schubert 2020) instead of the cultural anchoring of inequality through habitus and subtle distinction (Bourdieu 1984) and the importance of their strategic use for maintaining the social status quo, or to target the idea of hoardability and accumulation inherent in the concept of capital. Resource theory therefore reinforces the argument of the transformability of types of capital/resources, because a considerable endowment of resources often leads to the endowment of further or other resources, which tends to lead to the stability of inequality structures.

In addition to taking the importance of each individual resource into account, *Resource Theory* takes a particular look at the transformations of certain resource types into other resource types, which are based on very different inequality mechanisms (Knecht 2012c, 2011). For example, statistically speaking, higher education is also associated with higher income and better health (on these mechanisms in the context of *Resource Theory*, cf. Knecht 2012c: 53f., 2011: 591). Conversely, poor health leads to lower income (see ibid.). The connection between mental resources and health is discussed, among other things, within the framework of the salutogenesis approach (Knecht 2012c: 58). The social coping approach in turn shows how social resources have an effect on health (see for transformations Knecht/Schubert 2020: 314; Knecht 2012c: 165f., 2011: 591, 2010).

Since resources – and the scope for action they open up – are socially unequally distributed, *Resource Theory* functions as a *theory of social inequality* (Knecht 2010, 2011; Knecht/Schubert 2020) and is thus connected to other sociological theories: Giddens (1995) uses the concept of resources in structuration theory, distinguishing between allocative resources, which denote access to as well as appropriation of and use of natural livelihoods and material objects, and authoritative resources, which describe control over other actors and thus emphasise the meaning of relativity (see also Knecht/Schubert 2020: 310). In his "political sociology of social inequality", Kreckel (2004) connects this distinction by Giddens with Bourdieu's theory of types of capital. On the one hand, he cites two 'aggregate states' of inequality – unequal distribution of goods and asymmetrical relations (ibid.: 19). On the other hand, he develops a system of four 'strategic resources' (ibid.: 20): material wealth, symbolic knowledge, position in hierarchical organisations and participation or membership in a "selective association" referring to Marx's and Weber's concept of class. According to Kreckel, the first two resources are distributed (in an absolute way), while the latter two (representing two aspects of Bourdieu's social capital) lead to relational inequality, i.e. are not to be understood as 'more' or 'less' but as 'above' and 'below'. Therborn formulates three different inequalities: Resource inequality (income and education), vital (health) inequality, and a third type of inequality, existential inequality. The latter deals with the "unequal allocation of personhood, i.e., of autonomy, dignity, degrees of freedom, and of the right to respect and self-development" (Therborn 2013: 49). With their conception, the various authors aim at the potentiality of resources and their significance for the structuring of social inequality in society. The availability of these resources creates socially unequally distributed opportunities. At the same time, the authors use their distinctions to make it clear that in addition to the inequality of the (absolute) endowment with resources, questions of (relative) hierarchisation, distribution of power and unequal recognition must not be lost sight of (see also Knecht/Schubert 2020).

The unequal distribution of resources analysed by the various authors refers, on the one hand, to those resources that individuals have at their direct disposal or have generated themselves (through resource endowment and individual transformation) and, on the other hand, to those resources that they have received through society or through others. Therefore, inequality of distribution also depends on socio-political structures. For example, it has been shown that multi-unit, early-tracking, highly segmented school systems not only moderate social inequalities, but also reinforce and produce them (e.g. Becker/Lauterbach 2016). Cross-country comparisons show that countries that strive rather for social equality – such as the Scandinavian countries – tend to support weaker pupils, whereas those countries that emphasise inequalities in school performance – e.g. through grading, selection in transitions to secondary schools and separation of "elites" – perpetuate and reinforce inequality (see e.g. Becker and Lauterbach 2016; Solga 2014; Allmendinger/Leibfried 2003; see for discussion in the context of the resource approach: Knecht 2016: 849; Knecht/Schubert 2020: 317). In the resource-theoretical approach, I therefore try to conceptually highlight inequality-theoretical and socio-political questions to visualise the ways in which different resource endowments may come about. In particular, the multi-level approach examines how the different types of resources are allocated through processes at the structural level (macro-level) and institutional level (meso-level) and how they are developed and distributed at the individual level (micro-level).

Thus, with the help of the *Resource Theory* presented here, questions of justice can also be discussed in a new way (Knecht 2012b). In the philosophical discourse, questions of justice are still discussed today in the categories of exchange justice and distributive justice following Aristotle. From the perspective of *Resource Theory*, other questions arise: What about educational justice, if education is given to those who already have many resources? What about health equity when people with low incomes have a life expectancy that is up to ten years shorter than that of people with high incomes? What about equity when living in deprived neighbourhoods is associated with environmental burdens that are harmful to health, such as increased particle and noise pollution, or with other, more complex socio-ecological impairments? What about social capital equity, in the event that the multi-tiered school system (of the German-speaking countries) plays its part in splitting society into people with many opportunities and resources and people with few opportunities and resources, who have little interaction with each other? A contribution of *Resource Theory* to the philosophy of justice or social ethics could thus consist in a critique of theories of justice. For example, the notion of a just minimum endowment by Rawls (2005) strongly focuses on the importance of monetary resources for the establishment of justice. Walzer's notion of separate spheres of justice (Walzer 1998: 49) needs to be rethought in light of the strong correlations between different resources.

2.3 Resource Theory (IMTM) as a socio-political theory

With the interrelationships discussed above, *Resource Theory* (IMTM) *as a socio-political theory* refers to the (socio)political processes that determine the occurrence of resource distribution (Knecht 2012b; Knecht/Schenk 2023). The multilevel approach describes the political processes that influence the distribution of resources.[15] In political processes at the macro level (politics), for example, ideas of justice and legitimacy are "cast in form" through laws and decrees, which determine the institutional design or the further development of institutions. Social policy measures are then implemented within the framework of institutional regulations at the meso level (policy), e.g. concretised as service provision – whereby resources are allocated or the provision of resources is determined. In Figure 1, however, other areas of society are also mentioned that are significantly involved in the distribution or allocation of resources: on the one hand markets or companies, which are regulated, for example, by labour (protection) law, and on the other hand families, which themselves distribute resources in many ways, but are also themselves subject to a variety of legal regulations (Knecht 2010: 220f.).

The *Resource Theory* represents an extension of Bourdieu's theory of types of capital, among other things because of the broader spectrum of resources taken into account (cf. Schubert/Knecht 2012b; Knecht 2010) but also an extension of Amartya Sen's capability approach (Knecht 2012a, 2010), which focuses on income, education and life expectancy (as indicators of health) as inequality indicators. Sen's *capabilities* (and *functionings*) describe the possible uses or transformations of (material) resources into scope for action, whereby *functionings* describe individual possible uses, and *capabilities* are

---

15 On multilevel models, see also: Finis Siegler 2018; Boeckh et al. 2015b; Knecht/Schubert 2020; Knecht 2010.

Figure 1: Multi-level model of Resource Theory (IMTM)

Discourses on socio-political topics	Macro level
Political Conflicts (politics)	
Welfare/social policy (policy)	

Living conditions (incl. legal regulations)

1) Public institutions of education and health care, social work and other resource-allocating institutions	2) Companies, markets, income politics, occupational health and safety, consumer protection, etc. regulate the social exchange of resources	3) Relationships as a source of resources: family/friends/acquaintances: Provision of education, social capital and psychological resources

Meso level

co-production: citizen–state or professional–user of social services

Interaction

Micro level:
- income (economic capital)
- psychological/mental resources
- time / space
- health
- being educated (cultural capital)
- social capital

Source: Own representation based on Knecht 2010: 218.

bundles of such functionings, which – figuratively speaking – represent achievable spaces or – mathematically speaking – matrices (Knecht 2010, 2012a: 62f.). Individuals can use the resources to shape their lives in the way they consider valuable (see also Acconcia et al. 2017: 252; Sen 1999). In contrast, the (external) conversion factors represent, among other things, structural/society-dependent background variables that influence the importance and use of individual resources (Knecht 2012a: 67).

The capability approach is fruitful on an abstract level, as it represents a shift from the discussion of redistribution of material goods prevailing in the philosophy of justice towards the question of the social conditions of action and emphasises the importance of education and educational inequality in the discussion of justice. However, the operationalisation of *functionings*, *capabilities* and *conversion factors* has proven problematic:

While Sen presents individual *functionings* and *capabilities* in various texts, a complete description of possibilities for action proves to be almost impossible. Furthermore, Sen describes various dimensions and conditions of freedoms on a macro-level[16], failing, however, to establish a concrete relationship to individual *capabilities* (ebd; Knecht 2012c). He claims that democratic processes should determine which *functionings* (and resources) should be considered in social and political contexts (Sen 1999; cf. Robeyns 2005: 106). This is important and comprehensible for practical application, but it should not constitute a ban on thinking regarding scientific application in the sense that approaches that are comprehensible from a scientific point of view, but possibly not (yet) discussed socially, are excluded a priori (cf. Knecht 2012a). If the participatory involvement of those affected can be a meaningful strategy – e.g. also in participatory research and action research – social research should also be able to develop questions e.g. from research itself. *Resource Theory* (IMTM) thus represents a necessary concretisation and further development of the capability approach through 1.) an interdisciplinary, multidimensional view of resources, 2.) a focus on the transformation of resources to investigate inequality-generating and inequality-maintaining mechanisms, as well as through 3.) a multi-level view to link (socio)political processes with their concrete impact (ebd; Knecht 2012c, 2011).

Aspects of the *Resource Theory* presented here have already been received and applied in different empirical contexts: Metz (2016) uses the resource approach to examine the consequences of migration from Russia in a sociological analysis. Finis Siegler (2018) uses the multi-level approach to discuss the delivery context of social economy. Rose (2018) uses it to discuss the importance of the reproductive regime. Röh (2013: 231f.) uses aspects of the theory, in particular the idea of resource transformation, to develop a justice approach to

---

16 Sen lists freedom of expression, economic freedoms such as free access to markets, and access to education, health and basic social security as "freedoms" (Knecht 2011: 589, 2010: 53).

social work and thus takes up the approach of describing social work action within the framework of the *Resource Theory* (Knecht/Schubert 2012; Schubert/Knecht 2012a).

2.4 Resource Theory (IMTM) in social work

The *Resource Theory* developed here shows itself to be compatible with resource orientation, which is regarded as an essential conceptual guiding principle of social work.[17] Dieter Röh (2012), for example, takes a look at three theories in his remarks on the concept of resources in social work: The lifeworld orientation according to Thiersch (Thiersch/Grunwald/Köngeter 2012), the emergent systems theory (e.g. Staub-Bernasconi 2018), and the socio-ecological theory (e.g. Germain/Gitterman 2021). Röh shows that the theorisation of social work in its history was already strongly oriented towards the needs of the clients, which represents a form of resource orientation, and that such a viewpoint also found a counterpoint in social work that was mainly concerned with the adaptation of its clientele to social requirements. In the concept of *lifeworld orientation,* central resources for living one's one life are recognised in the certainties of action, relationships and routines of everyday life, but also in the antagonistic pressures (cf. Thiersch/Grunwald/Köngeter 2012; Thiersch 2014). However, this is linked with the criticism of a technocratic "resource management" without a concept of resources being formulated in detail (cf. Röh 2012). According to Staub-Bernasconi social work encompasses a wide range of social problems and she understands "the development of resources" as its "oldest method" (Staub-Bernasconi 2018: 316), which focuses on problems of "physical endowment (disease, epidemics, disabilities, anorexia such as obesity ...), socio-economic endowment (educational hardship/job suffering, the problems of the 'working poor' ...)" and "socio-ecological endowment (human-wasting workplace conditions, lack of or unreasonable as well as inadequate socio-spatial infrastructure in the field of health, work, physical and psychological security ...)" (ibid.: 273). Staub-Bernasconi points to the overly broad use of the concept of resources without, however, restricting its use herself (ibid.: 317). Thus, in her work, the term remains shimmering between an economic definition and a broader understanding. In the further development of Geiser's (2015) approach, the concept of resources is more closely aligned with Antonovsky.

The socio-ecological theory formulated as a "life model" by Germain/Gitterman (2021) is essentially based on the stress research of Lazarus/Folkman

---

17 This section largely follows the presentation in Knecht and Schubert 2012: 312–313 and 316.

(1984) and the socio-ecological research of Bronfenbrenner (1981). Life management is understood as a socio-ecological interaction between the demands and resources of the individual and the environment, whereby demands and resources are in a complementary relationship. Life management, developmental transitions and satisfaction of needs are thus to be understood as a continuous coping process for which the person needs individual and environmental resources. Here, too, there is a strong connection to psychological resource theories. However, in this approach "the political impetus of a resource orientation [...] tends to be lost" (Röh 2012: 197). Wendt (2010) takes the socio-ecological concept of resources further. In his eco-social theory, resources are "assets" that should be used by both the individual and the community for human well-being and should also be nurtured (Schubert 2013). This happens in social work "both as individually effective resource work and through supra-individually effective resource management" (Röh 2012: 198). The transactional resource concept of Schubert (2016) takes up these socio-ecological approaches and formulates them on the basis of a stress-management model of the interdependence of lifestyle and resource use.

Whereas resource orientation describes a fundamental attitude of social work action (Möbius/Friedrich 2010), intervention-related techniques such as work on the personal networks (Straus 2012), resource-oriented counselling (Schubert/Rohr/Zwicker-Pelzer 2019) or resource activation (Schubert 2021a) are methods that are based on a complex resource perspective and include different types of resources and their interactions.[18] Resource diagnostics records which resources are present in an individual and in his or her social and material/economic environment (Schubert 2021b; Glemser/Gahleitner 2012; Buttner/Knecht 2009).

The concepts presented suggest that the different resource approaches should be brought together across disciplines to make the _interdisciplinary, multidimensional, transformational and multi-level resource theory_ or _Resource Theory (IMTM)_ usable as an umbrella concept of understanding the meaning of resources in social work. The use of the concept of resources and the already broad reception of various resource concepts and references also show a high connectivity in social work. However, in some places the references to the concepts remain less transparent and systematic, in some cases they are not even made explicit (cf. Möbius/Friedrich 2010). The concept of resources itself also appears to be inconsistent and theoretically little elaborated. Against this background, it is worth bringing together the different theoretical strands.

The field of social work can also be aptly described with an elaborate concept of resources. For problems that are linked to the loss of individual

---

18 See specifically on resource endowment in and resource work with young people: Eberhard 2012; Sabatella/Wyl 2018; Dommermuth 2008; Düggeli 2009 and Drilling 2004.

resources, help is usually available from specialised professional groups such as doctors, psychotherapists, teachers or tax advisors, while responsibility for multidimensional problems, i.e. when resources from several relevant dimensions are affected, is often seen in social work.[19] Social work is particularly in demand when the socio-political distribution or allocation of resources is not provided solely through monetary benefits, but face-to-face through a psychosocial process (Knecht 2012b: 85). This results in an interdisciplinary and multidimensional reference to resources in social work.

For social work, taking transformability into account means that the whole spectrum of resources, including their interactions, must be considered (Knecht/Schubert 2020: 316). Social work counselling of the unemployed, for example, must not refrain from including not only material and social problems, but also the psychological problems of those affected (cf. Knecht 2016; Klevenow/Knecht 2013). If resource-oriented work succeeds, the development and interaction of personal, external and economic resources is sustainably set in motion (Knecht/Schubert 2020: 316). Often, resources only emerge when interacting: A stable relationship of trust and recognition is a necessary basis for building self-efficacy and motivation in clients. In an assessment or in profiling at the beginning of a counselling process, a resource situation can therefore be determined only provisionally (ibid.). For analyses in the field of social work, taking several levels into account also means asking where structural exclusion of resources, resource use and resource transfers take place. By looking at resources, inequality and hierarchisation can be brought into view: In addition to material poverty, problematic relations of recognition and their effects on psychological/mental resources, for example, must also be taken into account (Fabris et al. 2018). Personal problems and inadequately successful lifestyles must not be understood solely as the effect of personal deficits or as deviant behaviour on the part of the individual (see also Acconcia et al. 2017: 252; Schubert 2016). In terms of interventions, taking multiple levels into account means understanding the importance of processes at the political level for clients and, if necessary, intervening at this level as well. Concepts such as political empowerment (Herriger 2014) the triple mandate[20], the discussions of other social work mandates (e.g. Röh 2013) and the reception of concepts such as policy practice (see also Burzlaff/Eifler 2018; Rieger 2016) perpetuate the political claim that has always accompanied social work, namely the intention to improve the social conditions and socio-political circumstances that are partly responsible for the problems of their clients. However, this work does not only require social workers who are aware of the importance of the framework conditions of their clients' lives and of their own professional actions (Staub-Bernasconi 2018) but also corresponding organisations that implement

---

19 Schubert/Knecht 2012a: 10; Knecht 2012b: 85; Knecht/Schubert 2020: 316.
20 ... including the mandates of the client, the state and the profession (Staub-Bernasconi 2018).

such approaches. In this respect – following the *resource dependence theory* (e.g. Neumayr 2012) – the resources of (social) institutions must be questioned. The question of the enforceability of *weak interests* also refers to the importance of power processes and corresponding power resources (Ostheim/Schmidt 2007). The concept of resources presented here also forms a bridge between social work concepts of resources and power resource theories of interest enforcement (Knecht/Schubert 2020).

2.5 Understanding the mechanisms of resource distribution by analysing discourses and institutions – the role of political guiding principles and mission statements

It has been shown how the life situations of individuals can be described or assessed using an elaborated resource concept, the *Resource Theory (IMTM)*. The resource endowment of an individual depends on the allocation of resources by the persons and organisations in the environment, which takes place by means of various types and forms of human-environment interactions. The question of how the distribution, redistribution and allocation of resources occurs in political processes is of great importance. Within the framework of the multi-level model, the *Resource Theory* developed here looks at distribution-relevant (socio-political) discourses on the one hand; on the other hand, it examines the concrete institutions and mechanisms of distribution and allocation (Knecht 2010: chapter 3 and 4). Discourses and institutions are not to be understood as two different realities, but as different parts of social reality that can be analysed in different ways (Reckwitz 2016; Opielka 2005b).

With reference to Foucault, discourse is not understood as the linguistic representation of reality, but rather as the reality of language and linguistic representation (Hajer 2008: 212; Knecht 2010: 157). "A dialectical relationship emerges between discourses and the social structure forming their context: both act reciprocally as conditions and effects. Discourses constitute the world – and conversely they are also constituted; they (re)produce and transform society; they perform the construction of social identities, the production of social relations between persons and the construction of systems of knowledge and belief" (Keller 2004: 28; s. a. Diaz-Bone 2018). Discourses hold fundamental conceptions of the world. Established discourses represent *orders* of knowledge (Keller 2006: 126) that are difficult to question.

Within the framework of *Resource Theory*, the focus is on the significance of discourses in the distribution of resources. An analytical distinction can be made between different levels. In discourses *on the macro-level*, such as the topics of the mass media and parliamentary debates, fundamental decisions are made that help to determine the socio-political distribution of resources (Knecht 2010: 161). Studies *on macro-level discourses* also deal, for example, with attitudes of political elites, organisational cultures or socio-political implementation research (cf. chapter 3.2 below). *At the meso level*, for example, adopted laws, ordinances, decrees, etc. (all of which are recorded in the form of language!) are implemented, whereby the organisations have room for manoeuvre ("discretion" of the street-level bureaucracy; Lipksy 1980). The scientific and professional discourses that are received and partly produced by the professionals are an essential part of the meso-level discourses (cf. chapter 3.3). The meso level also has an effect on the macro level through the definition and description of problems. At the micro level, discourses come into play, for example, in the communication between clients and employees in social institutions or at public offices. Here the question arises which ideas professionals have about the realities of the clients' lives or how these clients feel to be perceived (cf. below, chapter 3.4.).

For the development of a theory of resources that focuses on socio-political processes, the reconstruction of discourses is important because (socio-political) discourses not only determine which resources are due to whom and how they should be distributed, but also because discourses determine which resources or which aspects of resources have which importance or appear to be particularly important. For example, the importance of education has changed greatly in the last twenty years. Studies such as the PISA study can be seen as an indicator that education and education policy are increasingly seen as part of social policy (Opielka 2005a; Finkeldey 2007). Unequal education is seen as a central mechanism of reproducing social inequality and equal educational opportunities as a way to curb increasing income and wealth inequality. Therefore, social policies and educational activities increasingly focus on the development of early childhood skills and competencies in order to improve future employment prospects and ensure the sustainable integration of young people into the labour force (Atzmüller/Décieux/Knecht 2019: 108). In the context of this change, the understanding of education is also changing, as activities are shaped by the concepts of competence building, employability and human capital formation, which are seen as a means to align productivity and competitiveness with social inclusion (ibid.).

In the context of this paper, the approaches relevant in (social) policy discourses – such as the social investment approach, activation policy and neoliberalism – are considered as guiding principles ("Leitbilder") or mission models and analysed in the context of a resource-theoretical allocation policy. Guiding principles represent types of attitudes, values and related policies (ibid.; see also below). They focus on certain principles of justice (such as distributive justice, needs-based justice, merit-based justice, productivist justice, exclusionary justice, etc.; cf. Ebert 2015) and justify positions on social policy areas or model topics (familialism, scope of care and insurance benefits, equality policy, accuracy, activation, obligation, conditionality of aid, discrimination, participation, economisation, dualization/hierarchisation, privatisation; cf. Boeckh et al. 2015a). Guiding principles can represent different aspects of political processes. Thus, mental guiding principles (as patterns of imagination) can be distinguished from manifest (verbalised) principles, as can abstract, propagated and idea-dominated guiding principles from guiding principles in practised models (see Fig. 2.).

Figure 2: Overview of guiding principles

Appearance / Effectiveness in work		Mental guiding principles (patterns of imagination)	Manifest guiding principles (verbalised)
Propagated guiding principles (desirable, potential)	self-supported	Ideas with mission statement potential (e.g. politics/discourse analysis on intentional politics)	Explicit mission statements (e.g. party programmes)
	external	imposed guiding principles	
Guiding principles in practice (internalised, guiding action)		Implicit guiding principles (e.g. policy analysis on realised policy)	Explicit guiding principles (e.g. policy analysis of policy formulated through legislation)

Source: Own representation based on Giesel 2007: 39.

Policy analyses often use guiding principles to typify policies in practice. For example, various authors divide social policy approaches into different models. For example, Morel et al. (2012) and Leibetseder (2016) divide policy approaches into "Keynesian social policy", "neoliberal social policy" and "social investment". Boeck et al. (2015a) distinguish between economically liberal, compensatory and activating welfare states; Laruffa (2018) distinguishes between neoliberal social policy and the social investment approach and the capability approach. However, terms such as neoliberalism are also used in the policy itself. Therefore, it must be noted that scientifically reconstructed guiding principles are related to the guiding principles of political discourses, but are not congruent (see Fig. 2 and Giesel 2007). A look at the difference between discursively disseminated mission statements (e.g. in election programmes and public statements) and the guiding principles reconstructed from the observation of political practice can point to typical implementation patterns and problems as well as to actively or offensively used strategies of concealment.

Compared to a classification with the help of welfare regimes, analyses of guiding principles are predominantly focused on political discourses or the relations of political discourses to institutional changes. This makes them more suitable for observing and explaining short-term changes. In the following, four central academic guiding principles of current policy analyses are presented and briefly introduced as central scientific mission statements of current policy analyses: (1) neoliberalism, (2) social investment, (3) the capability approach (CA) and (4) the right-wing populist/extreme-right social policy mission statement. The different models place different resources in the foreground of their considerations and focus on different mechanisms of resource allocation.

(1) Neoliberalism. The term neoliberalism stands for a "doctrine that has emerged since the 1930s that absolutizes the market as a regulatory mechanism of social development and decision-making processes" (Butterwegge/Lösch/Ptak 2008: 9). In political research, however, the term and the concept of neoliberalism have only played a greater role since the mid-1990s. In research, too, there is no single neoliberal approach, but a rather multitude of thinkers whose ideas and attitudes overlap. The politics of neoliberalism are characterised by the liberalisation of market-based regulations, privatisation, the globalisation of markets, the economisation of administration and criticism of welfare state security. Unlike the "old" liberal policies of the 19th century, "neo"-liberal policies do not consist in a retreat from the market and a dismantling of statehood, but in extending market logic to all spheres of society and providing the framework for people's actions (cf. Fischer 2020: 380; see also Foucault 2004; Hammerschmidt 2014). Accordingly, as already mentioned above, neoliberal reform projects, such as in Great Britain under Margaret Thatcher or in Germany under Gerhard Schröder ("Hartz IV"-reform in 2002–2005), did not so much have a dismantling of the welfare state in mind, but rather a change in wage relations and the re-commodification of labour power through a far-reaching "neo-social" (see above) transformation of individuals and their ability to work (Atzmüller 2014; Jessop 2018; Bröckling 2007).

From the perspective of *Resource Theory*, the narrowing of the neoliberal image of man to the supposedly calculating and self-interested character of man – in the sense of "homo oeconomicus" – is central (Ptak 2008). According to this idea, people can be controlled primarily by financial incentive mechanisms. Therefore, the distribution mechanisms of material resources (and especially the design of financial incentives) are at the forefront of neoliberal policies. In self-descriptions of neoliberalism, the focus is on the alleged efficiency of financial incentive mechanisms, which are to be used in more and more social sub-sectors organised along market lines and would thus solve efficiency problems of all kinds. As already mentioned, the market is seen as having a quasi-pedagogical function. Therefore, people who are assumed not to be sufficiently controlled by the market are activated and disciplined. Thus, the unemployed – under the assumption that there must be enough jobs, if only wages were flexible enough – are accused of being too demanding and inactive.

Measures such as cuts in transfer benefits, a stricter sanctions regime and the activation of job placements oriented towards the work-first principle aim to secure the work ethic of the unemployed and to (re)integrate them better into the flexible and precarious segments of the labour markets. (Atzmüller/Décieux/Knecht 2019: 111; Stelzer-Orthofer/Weidenholzer 2011). In the European version of neoliberalism, workers in particular are increasingly exposed to markets or quasi-markets ("commodification"), while companies are granted locational advantages through positive incentives such as subsidies.

A resource-theoretical view of neoliberalism also addresses the distributive consequences of neoliberal/neosocial policies as well as the psychological burdens and effects on psychological/mental resources. For example, the social and emotional consequences of the marketisation of society and the threatening and sanctioning measures of neoliberal policies, understood as activation, must also be kept in view and the question must be raised whether – viewed comprehensively – they do not themselves lead to suboptimal results (even in the sense of neoliberal goals).

(2) The concept of social investment was propagated in reaction to the establishment of neoliberal thinking and its penetration of political and public discourse, first by the British Labour Party and then by other, mainly social democratic, parties in Europe; central to this was Giddens' work "The Third Way" Giddens 2000). The concept quickly found its way into the rest of Europe (Leibetseder 2016) – among other things through the basic paper published in June 1999 by the two chancellors Tony Blair and Gerhard Schröder (Schroeder/Blair 1999). Social investment policies (Kohlrausch 2014; Solga 2012) aim to make social policy more effective: through measures such as improving "human capital" through training and qualification, through the promotion of research and development as well as through the expansion of childcare (Esping-Andersen et al. 2002; Hemerijck 2013; cf. Knecht 2011). Proponents of the social investment concept claim to be able to reconcile (assumed) economic requirements (e.g. securing competitiveness) and social needs so that they mutually promote each other. The expansion of childcare shoud, among others, improve women's opportunities to participate in the labour force. However, the measures are justified in particular by the need to ensure that children

and young people from disadvantaged families (in terms of access to education and the labour market) can be educated as early as possible ("early promoting state"; in German: "Frühförderstaat"; Knecht 2011), but also throughout childhood and youth (Knecht 2012c) as this is considered to be the best way to avoid unemployment, poverty and criminality later on (Esping-Andersen 2008).

In fact, in Austria, too, a policy has recently prevailed in which entitlements are reduced and transfer payments are linked to the counter-performance of the unemployed in order to increase their allegedly low willingness to participate in the labour force (Atzmüller 2014, 2009; Atzmüller/Krenn/Papouschek 2012). Critical studies of these developments point above all to the repressive tendencies of activating transformations and reconfigurations of social policy (Gray 2004; Wyss 2010). They identify these tendencies as a prerequisite for far-reaching processes of recommodification of the commodity labour power through flexibilization and precarisation (Scherschel/Streckeisen/Krenn 2012; Pelizzari 2009), which are associated with changes in the government of the subjects (Lessenich 2012; Bröckling/Krasmann/Lemke 2000).

From a *Resource Theory* perspective, social investment policy can be understood as a policy that focuses in particular on the resource education. However, education is limited to its functional significance for income generation: employability (Kraus 2007). As far as the distribution of resources and patterns of inequality is concerned, the social investment concept is often associated with hopes for an improvement in equal opportunities through higher participation in education – however, the logic of the investment calculus corresponds to a concentration on worthwhile investments. This can lead to a stronger focus on meritocratic logics to legitimise inequality and selective access to different educational pathways (Müller 2015; Solga 2005). According to this logic, all individuals should be given (formal) access to educational activities, but at the same time this access remains selective and, in the context of increased human capital orientation, is primarily geared towards marketability (Atzmüller/Knecht 2017a). Social investment activities are then primarily directed towards those groups of people who prove themselves in terms of meritocratic logic and who succeed in building a more or less stable life based on employment histories; other groups are also denied support if necessary (cf. Büschken 2017). In particular, recipients of so-called "unproductive measures/ interventions" (e.g. pension payments, care for the elderly) run the risk of having to cope with reduced benefits.

Although the guiding principle of the social investment state has repeatedly been presented as an alternative to neoliberal policies, there are nevertheless overlaps between the two models (cf. Hemerijck 2013; Morel/Palier/Palme 2012; critical: Cantillon 2011). In particular, it became apparent that the social investment concept is also characterised by activating measures (Atzmüller/Knecht 2017a; Peck 2001). In Germany in particular, the restructuring of the welfare state was – at least superficially – driven forward along the slogan "demanding and supporting" (in German: "fordern und fördern"), which can be translated in terms of content as "activation policy within the framework of a social investment approach".

Analyses of these developments emphasise that ideas of individual self-responsibility, which can best be realised by pursuing one's own interests on the (labour) markets, are linked with ideas according to which the working capacity of individuals represents a human capital whose permanent change and adaptation mutates into a moral requirement in the context of self-responsible subjectivity. This conception of the subject, which focuses on adult, 'mature' individuals, is shaped by certain expectations of rationality, which are based on ideas of the *entrepreneurial self* (Bröckling 2007; Rose 2000) as an updated version of the individual utility maximiser (Foucault 2004) capable of acting autonomously and freely in the marketplace (cf. Atzmüller/Knecht 2017a).

(3) The third central guiding principle is the *Capability Approach* (CA), which goes back to the philosophers Amartya and Martha Nussbaum. It has already been discussed above as the starting point of the resource approach; however, it can also be seen as a socio-political model developed from theory, which is often referred to in the academic discourse of educational science, social pedagogy and social work (see footnote 22). Capabilities refer to the amount of room for manoeuvre that people have at their disposal (overview: Knecht 2010: chapter 2.2, 2012a). The extent of scope for action is described as being equally dependent on individual characteristics (e.g. skills and competences, physical and monetary resources) as well as on social circumstances (Knecht 2011; Kuklys 2005: 11). With reference to development policy considerations, Sen discusses political and economic freedoms, "social opportunities" such as those provided by education and health care, more extensive basic security through social insurance, among other things, as well as protection against arbitrariness and corruption.[21] Although elements of social policy are hereby presented as essential for the individual's scope of action, political measures to create them are discussed neigher in sufficient detail nor concretely within Sen and Nussbaum's original approach. While Martha Nussbaum presented a list of desirable basic freedoms (Nussbaum 1999: 57) of which, however, not all are socio-politically accessible, Sen pointed out that the question which capabilities should be improved by society in which way should be answered within democratic processes (Sen 1999). Already in the formative phase of the CA, Sen pointed out that philosophies of justice should be called into question on the basis of their *informational basis of judgement of justice* (abbr.: IBJJ) (Sen 1990; see also Knecht/Kuchler/Atzmüller 2014; Atzmüller/Knecht 2017a; Sen 1999; Otto et al. 2017). Depending on which aspect is brought to the fore (such as equality of opportunity, distribution,

---

21 Sen 1999; overview and discussion: Knecht 2010: 53f.

capabilities, benefits, resources, satisfaction of basic needs, subjective satisfaction, distributional outcomes), judgments of justice arrive at different results.

Before CA was received and further developed in educational science and social pedagogical research[22], it has served as an approach to justice philosophy and development policy (Robeyns 2005). By addressing the importance of public institutions for the empowerment of individuals (Sen 1999), the CA opened up the socio-political discussion of the philosophy of justice to the question regarding the significance of policy-making and youth policy have for the concrete opportunities of every individual young person (Knecht/ Kuchler/Atzmüller 2014). Especially in the transition to adult or working life, inequalities between young people manifest themselves in a limitation of educational opportunities, e.g. due to a lack of resources and offers or discrimination (see below). Social crises further reduce the choices and opportunities of disadvantaged young people (Sting 2011: 40). This connection can be well illustrated within the framework of Sen's capability approach (see e.g. Knecht 2014; Knecht/Kuchler/Atzmüller 2014). In addition, the CA also offers references to the importance of democracy, participation, co-determination, empowerment, and the development of a sense of community (see also Knecht 2014) and autonomy (cf. Bothfeld 2017; Betzelt/Bothfeld 2014).[23]

(4) The fourth model is the right-wing populist/extreme right model of an *exclusion-oriented social policy*. Many of the European right-wing populist/ extreme right parties originally advocated authoritarian-neoliberal positions

---

22   On the development of the CA's relationship to the educational sciences: Walker 2005; Otto/Schrödter 2007; Otto/Ziegler 2010a; Otto/Ziegler 2010b; Röh 2013; Clark/Ziegler 2016; Otto et al. 2017; Okkolin et al. 2018; Otto/Walker/Ziegler 2018.
23   From a resource theory perspective, the capability approach also has some weak points: The fact that capabilities describe "doings and things" at the same time leads to ambiguities as to whether they are intended to describe the use of resources or possible outcomes of actions (for a critique, see also Knecht 2010: 67). Secondly, as already mentioned, there is a gap between his empirical studies with highly aggregated data and the theoretical argumentations strongly aimed at the individual person on the importance of resources as well as on the importance of the ability to use resources. This missing link can be called the micro-macro gap (Knecht 2011: 592). Thirdly, it is to be criticised that in his contributions he very strongly emphasises the ability to use resources, but in doing so loses sight of the importance of the resources themselves (ibid.). As mentioned above, this also corresponds to a weak point of various socio-political argumentations that rely on influencing inequality structures in the direction of greater social equality through educational policy measures alone (Solga 2012, 2014; Kohlrausch 2014). Fourth, he neglects to discuss power structures that lead to unequal distributions. His approach that more resources lead to greater agency (and freedom) is sociologically uninformed because it does not consider that more resources imply new distributional struggles and new methods of distinction (Knecht 2011: 592). Sen thus does not address the relational meaning of inequality.

(Hall 1986; Bruff 2013) and this is also how the current policies and projects of some right-wing governments, e.g. in Hungary, Poland, the Czech Republic or Slovenia, can be categorised (Atzmüller 2022, Lendvai-Bainton/Szelewa 2020; Stubbs/Lendvai-Bainton 2020). Various studies (Röth/Afonso/Spies 2018; Lefkofridi/Michel 2017) have shown that governments with authoritarian-populist participation (or tolerance) of the extreme right have not or hardly reduced the level of spending on social policy, but the quality of social policy measures has changed. Indeed, since the mid-1990s, various authoritarian-populist and extreme right parties have begun to develop independent social policy ideas to broaden their electoral basis (Swank/Betz 2019). This justifies considering a separate right-wing populist/extreme right social policy model. In social science debates, the socio-political programmes are often referred to as welfare chauvinism (Ennser-Jedenastik 2018a, 2016; Keskinen 2016). This refers to policies based on the belief that welfare state benefits should be primarily targeted at the 'native' group, defined by citizenship, ethnicity, race or religion. In contrast, members of the non-native out-group should receive limited, if any, social support (Fischer 2020). Ennser-Jedenastik (2016, 2018a) with reference to Austria, emphasises nativism in this context as the most important organising principle of extreme right social policy. In order to demonstrate this, the social policy changes must be seen in a broader context; it is not enough to look at the changes in individual measures. Thus Atzmüller/Knecht/Bodenstein (2020) point out that welfare chauvinist policies are often embedded in a broader authoritarian, right-wing elitist project that opposes emancipation and political participation, stands for renationalisation, and additionally fosters traditional family structures, gendered division of labour, pronatalist policies as well as punitive, educational and also explicitly exclusionary measures in a wide range of social policies (s. a. Biskamp 2019).[24]

This kind of policy-making can be combined with the repression of the democratic actors of civil society, the workers' movement and the social partners, as well as of the political and public control bodies (media, independent courts) while pushing an economic and national productivism that deepens inequalities and promotes the national middle classes (Atzmüller 2022). Right-wing populist and extreme right parties in various countries use the criticism of welfare state benefits (and especially those that benefit non-citizens) to discredit the welfare state as a whole and in this way legitimise and enforce the dismantling or restructuring of the welfare state (Fischer 2020). Social policy

---

[24] For Lehner and Wodak (2020) right-wing populism includes, first, nationalism/nativism/anti-pluralism, second, anti-establishment/anti-elitism, third, authoritarianism/hierarchical society and, fourth, conservatism/historical revisionism. This position goes back to the discussion of the 1930s and 1940s about the "authoritarian character" who wants to be part of a strong, authority-led collective, which, however, can only be established through demarcation from an imagined "other" (Biskamp 2019: 97). This attitude is related to the advocacy of punitive and activist policies.

measures that aim at restricting freedoms by limiting individual gains in autonomy along national, religious as well as class- and gender-specific structures and cementing or deepening social inequalities are part of this strategy. The socio-political measures give shape to the conservative to extreme far-right ideas of gender, family and population policy intentions that justify them, which are usually underpinned by culturalist-racist or genetic-racist argumentations (Butterwegge 2018; Atzmüller 2022; Tálos 2006; Rosenberger/Schmid 2003). From a resource-theoretical point of view, this is not only about cutting benefits or allocating resources, but also explicitly about using measures (or deliberate inaction) beyond social policy to prevent people from using the resources they have.

Often, these reactionary policies enforce measures "designed to discipline (or at best incentivise) poor people's behaviour through segregated (and low-quality) delivery systems, often in punitive ways" (Fischer 2020: 381, translation: A.K.).[25] "This is regularly presented as promoting the rights of the poor, whereas this often does not correspond to the function of the measures actually implemented" (ebd; s. a. Biskamp 2019). Alongside the disciplining of one population group (e.g. the unemployed or those affected by poverty) are policies that do not discipline people but push them to the margins of society (Atzmüller 2022). Examples of this marginalisation (Biskamp 2019: 100f.) which often goes hand in hand with spatial segregation, are the banishment of people to camps such as asylum camps or deportation centres, but also marginalisation on the labour market, e.g. through the establishment of substitute and secondary labour markets (e.g. special labour markets for seasonal workers, temporary work permits, 24-hour care, etc.), through the displacement of homeless people and beggars from the inner cities or also within the framework of a women-at-the-stove policy. In extreme cases, these exclusionary policies force the criminalisation of particularly disadvantaged groups of the population (e.g. homeless people in Hungary; see also Lindberg 2020). At the same time, the laws that are enacted within the framework of these policies are conspicuously often beyond the limits of what is legally permissible.[26]

Comparing the approaches, it can thus be said that the CA – similar to the neoliberal model – discusses access to markets as an expansion of individual opportunities, but it incorporates the importance of societal and socio-political circumstances in a very different way. Both the CA and the social investment approach the emphasis on education for the development and advancement of people. However, in the social investment approach, the importance of

---

25 "[S]uch interventionist and segregationist impulses [...] fit comfortably well with the similarly segregationist impulse of illiberal right-wing populism. While the latter targets its discipline at racial or other groups rather than generic categories of poor people, the fact that poverty is often racialized allows for a smooth transition between these two conceptual targets." (Fischer 2020: 381f.)
26 For Austria: Sallmuter 2002; Verfassungsgerichtshof 2021, 2019.

education is largely limited to its vocational usability for income generation (Bonvin/Galster 2010) whereas the CA discusses education in its functional meaning (also for democracy) as well as in its "intrinsic" meaning, i.e. as a value in itself. Sen sees the importance of increasing agency in its enabling people to pursue goals, "they have reason to value" (Sen 1999: 63). He thus clearly distances himself from the idea of activating measures, which are part of neoliberal and social investment measures.

The right-wing populist/extreme right ideology has some overlapping points with the neoliberal ideology, but differs strongly in the attitude towards migrants and asylum seekers, who are seen as potential workers in the neoliberal worldview and are seen as others to be excluded in the right-wing populist ideology. Mudde and Rovira Kaltwasser point out, however, that populism in general remains indeterminate with regard to many issues and therefore partly overlaps with other ideologies (Mudde/Rovira Kaltwasser 2019).

Resource theory provides the framework for the coming analysis. The focus is on the two areas: the analysis of discourses on the one hand and the institutional changes on the other one. The guiding principles serve to keep in mind the modes of allocation or the combination of policies of resource allocation. They thus establish a link between discourses and institutions. The field of employment promotion can be analysed as a network of the multidimensional allocation of educational resources, material resources, and psychological/mental resources (interdisciplinary). Institutional changes in the field of employment promotion accordingly also lead to changed individual constellations of resource endowments. The phase of finding a profession and entering the labour market can also be seen and analysed as a concretisation of the idea of transforming educational resources into monetary resources. The guiding principles listed above serve as a basis for the analysis of the change in discourses in institutions in the field of employment support for disadvantaged youth. The ideological content and meaning of fragments of discourses as well as individual measures and the change of these measures can be clarified in their overall context by assigning them to the guiding principles – and, if necessary, enables making fractures between widespread discourses and institutional analyses visible.

3 Changing discourses on labour market policies for youth and youth employment promotion

3.1 Notes on design and method

This paper sets out to answer the question how employment support for disadvantaged young people as part of social policy changed in Austria between 2000 and 2020 and what effects this change has had on the framework conditions of not only social pedagogues, social workers and other professionals working in this field but also on the young people themselves. In the following the change of relevant discourses (this chapter 3) the institutional changes during this period (chapter 4) are examined.

From a methodological point of view, the various projects on which this work is based represent interpretative policy analyses within the framework of policy field analyses. Policy field analyses, as opposed to formal policy processes, focus on the content of the practice of politics and are concerned with what political actors do, why they do it and what they achieve (see e.g. Blum/Schubert 2018; Schubert/Bandelow 2014). Interpretive policy analysis, as a qualitative method of policy research, emphasises the "reality-constructing dimension of ideas, knowledge, interpretive patterns, frames, interpretations, arguments or discourses in political processes" (Münch 2016: 2), and follows, according to Münch, the basic ideas that "social and political reality is socially and discursively constructed" and that "politics is a struggle for meanings" (ibid.: 3). Although e.g. legal texts, ordinances, etc., which are a constituting part of institutions, are also texts that can be interpreted discourse-analytically, discourses can nevertheless be distinguished from institutions and analysed separately (on the distinction, see also Reckwitz 2016).

In the various projects mentioned above, which form the basis of this paper, I have – in cooperation with colleagues and within the framework of critical discourse analyses (Blommaert/Bulcaen 2000; Wodak 2007) – analysed the argumentation and argumentative patterns of discourses and observed shifts in the discourse order and the enforcement of hegemonic discourses (Fairclough/Fairclough 2012). Sporadically, the metaphorical level of language has been considered.

As explained above, discourses can be examined at different levels (see above and Knecht 2010: 161). In the projects, discourses were analysed at three different levels; these will first be briefly introduced (see (1) to (3)) and then dealt with in more depth in the next three sub-chapters. (1) The public discourses of the government are of general importance, as they take place before and during controversial legislative processes or also during public presentations of new measures (mainly top-down). These discourses are often characterised by an intention to legitimise political plans and actions and are linked to public discourses on social policy, e.g. discourses on the misuse of welfare state benefits or on the importance and production of economic growth (see chapter 3.2). They legitimise certain ways of allocating and distributing resources in the public sphere. (2) In the projects – and especially in the SocIEtY project (see above, fn. 9) – were the discourses of experts employed in the administration and ministries were of particular interest (section 3.3). These *administrative-political discourses* (Blommaert/Bulcaen 2000: 451) play a central (also legitimising) role in the processes of legislation, the resulting legal norms of which form the basis for the actions of administrations, social institutions and also companies. In these discourses, professional argumentation plays a stronger role, but it is primarily the ministries that are faced with the task of translating argumentations and decisions for the above-mentioned public discourse. (3) In the work of professionals in the field (in addition to public, legal and implementation-related discourses), professional discourses – as *institutional discourses* – are particularly significant (ibid.). The perceptions of professionals, for example social workers and social pedagogues working "front-line" within the street-level bureaucracy, have an impact on the measures, on the way services are provided, and on the interactions with clients and thus have a direct influence on the allocation of resources (chapter 3.4). In the context of the analysis of interactions between professionals and clients, the question arises in which way the design of service provision (e.g. as an offer for young people described as deficient) is subjectivised by the young people. For example, young people in counselling or in other measures can subjectivise the world views transported or projected onto them (see also chapter 3.4).

Ultimately, by means of the discourses, the allocation of resources (in the sense of the *Resource Theory (IMTM)* to the young people is legitimised and partly also organised by different institutions. Chapter 4 therefore traces the institutional developments – following the analysis of the discourses.

3.2 Public discourses on youth unemployment and labour market policies for youth

It is often governments that make social benefits an issue in the public sphere and especially in the mass media, be it to highlight their own achievements, to launch promises or to legitimise cuts in the welfare state (Wogawa 2000; Oschmiansky/Schmid/Kull 2003; Uske 2000). Such discourses are partly oriented towards the various socio-political models presented above, which are brought into position against each other or against other argumentations. The topics are either initiated by interested parties or on the occasion of special events and then negotiated in public. In addition to more argumentative disputes, there are repeated waves of more polemical thematization of the abuse of benefits by allegedly "unworthy" benefit recipients or "social parasites" (Lehnert 2009; Oschmiansky/Schmid/Kull 2003; Uske 2000, 1995). In these discussions, the need to 'keep up' the work ethic in society is frequently emphasised (cf. Lehnert 2009: 89), while at the same time portraying it as endangered by ideas of widespread abuse of social benefits often plays a major role. Wogawa (2000) has shown in a comprehensive study how the discourse on the abuse of social benefits typically plays out: The existing control mechanisms to prevent abuse are ignored and the impression is given that a life close to the subsistence level and without work is desirable. The fraud of the (labour) administration is presented as low-threshold and self-evident. Control mechanisms are often called for, even where they already exist (ibid.). In the polemical discourses, images which stick in people's head are used: "shirkers", "unwilling to work", "scrounger", "asylum abusers" or even "parasites" are expressions of this discourse on benefit abuse (see for details Knecht 2010: 166f.). The allegedly high number of citizens abusing benefits is described as a central problem (Wogawa 2000; s. a. Knecht 2010: 163f.). In the following, I will analyse the public discourses on two topics as examples, both of which are related to disadvantaged young people and employment promotion. The first is the introduction of the training obligation, the second the disputes in the run-up to the reform of the minimum income scheme, which led to the reintroduction of the term social assistance in 2018.

While the introduction of the training guarantee in Austria in 2008 was not discussed controversially, the introduction of compulsory training and education in 2017 made greater demands on social legitimacy. On the part of the ministries that pushed for its introduction, primarily social investment arguments were put forward, which were also taken up by many media: Young people who would drop out of school or training and accept auxiliary jobs would have a "bad start into working life"; it would entail "lifelong serious consequences for those concerned" (BMAFJ 2016: 5). These young people have "a threefold risk of unemployment, a fourfold risk of becoming unskilled workers and a sevenfold risk of being unemployed" (ibid.). The expenditure related to the commitment was legitimised by the fact that young people who have further education or training reduce their risk of unemployment by two-thirds and that "through future sustainable, skilled employment [...] there will be more tax revenue and less expenditure on unemployment benefits and other social benefits" (ibid.: 18). When the compulsory training was presented to the public, a more economic argumentation came into play alongside the discussion focused more strongly on education policy and youth. The federal government emphasised that compulsory training should serve to secure growth and employment (BMASK 2015b; Federal Chancellery 2013) and that "we cannot afford and do not want to accept a 'lost generation'" (BMASK, n.d., as cited in Knecht/Atzmüller 2019: 221). It was "convinced that the project [...] would set a milestone in improving the level of education and the labour market opportunities of young people as well as in meeting the future demand for skilled workers of Austrian companies" (BMASK 2015a). In statements by the BMASK, after criticism of these proposals, a certain ambivalence towards the compulsory character of the measure became apparent. The compulsory character was emphasised in public statements by renaming the measure initially called "training obligation", "Training up to 18". (cf. Atzmüller/Knecht 2016a) In public relations, the now compulsory offer was presented as a new opportunity.

Overall, the discourse showed a strong affinity to the social investment approach (Knecht 2010; Atzmüller/Knecht 2017b). The measures were supported by the two coalition partners at the time, the social democratic SPÖ and the conservative ÖVP, albeit with different justifications. Within the framework of the social investment guideline, depending on the context and the addressee, the advantages for young people were emphasised more strongly, or the advantages for the economic system or the companies confronted with the shortage of skilled labour. The fact that the compulsory and punitive character of compulsory training has been pushed into the background by the government in public representations conveys the actually outdated image of a supportive, distributive welfare state and conceals its demanding character (Knecht/ Atzmüller 2019: 221).

A second controversial topic in the public discourse on the welfare state, which also affects young people, is the debate on social assistance. With the period under review, social assistance in Austria was reformed in 2010 and 2019. In 2010, the means-tested minimum income scheme was introduced. It was intended to address the shortcomings of the previously prevailing decentralised system, which was characterised by low take-up and a high degree of discretionary power of the local welfare bureaucracy (Fink/Leibetseder 2019). In this framework, social assistance was renamed "means-tested minimum income". The new reform of 2019 was placed in the framework of the refugee migration and asylum debate. Especially from 2015 onwards, the entire public debate on (social) policy was strongly influenced by this debate. Almost every issue was placed in this context; it constituted a "universal signifier" (Laclau/ Mouffe 1991). The high proportion of recognised refugees or refugees with subsidiary protection among minimum income recipients (approx. 35%), which is due to the fact that the labour market is only open to this group once the asylum procedure has been completed, was stylised as a problem that endangered the continued existence of the Austrian welfare state, even though expenditure on minimum income amounted to less than 1.5% of the total social expenditure in Austria[27] (on this and on the following argumentation, see Atzmüller/Knecht/Bodenstein 2020). Already in the government programme, the announced reform was predominantly presented as a measure to prevent "immigration into the social systems" (ibid.; Salzburger Nachrichten 2017; s. a. John 2017). It was justified with the argument that it could "not be that Austrians who have contributed all their lives get less or the same from the welfare state as immigrants who have only been living in Austria for a short time" (ÖVP/FPÖ 2017: 117). The implied claim that asylum-seeking migrants would receive the same benefits is, however, false insofar as recent immigrants do not have access to social security benefits and asylum-seekers, in particular, only had and have access to basic security benefits that are reduced compared to minimum security/social assistance. Nevertheless, the benefit entitlements of migrant families with many children in particular were subsequently scandalised by politicians of the coalition. Defining the high birth rate of Syrian and Afghan women to two decimal places ("3.91 per woman", cf. APA OTS 2018c), the parliamentary party leaders of the coalition parties argued in a joint press statement that the reform of means-tested minimum income would "counteract these developments" (ibid.). Their racist argument not only alluded to an alleged lack of work ethic among recent migrants. They also referred to the idea of "immigration into the social system" (ÖVP/FPÖ 2017: 117) and an "invasion" of migrants and asylum seekers, which had been spread by high-ranking politicians of the FPÖ (Kurier 2016b; Die Presse 2016). The claims of migrants and migrant families to receive benefits were presented as more or less illegitimate. According to this, migrants who were unwilling to integrate "looted" the welfare state (APA OTS 2018b) – "large foreign families [...] exploit [...] our social system to the hilt" (APA OTS 2018a; see also Atzmüller/Knecht/Bodenstein 2020.

When the government took office in December 2017, however, the attacks against asylum seekers were combined with attacks against Austrian benefit recipients. Allegedly, a large number of recipients of both groups were abusing the minimum benefits (Knecht/Atzmüller 2021). Two campaigns were initiated by the then Federal Chancellor Kurz: First, he claimed that "fewer and fewer people get up in the morning to work, and in more and more families only the children get up in the morning to go to school" (Chancellor Sebastian Kurz, as cited in Bauer 2021). He thus echoed the statements of former Chancellor Wolfgang Schüssel, who at the beginning of the first conservative/far-right "Black-Blue" Coalition in February 2000 announced in his government declaration that "[t]he abuse of state transfer payments [...] is unsocial and lacks solidarity. It must be stopped resolutely" (Rosenberger/Schmid 2003: 96). On the other hand, Chancellor Kurz stated that it "cannot be the task of

---

27 In 2019, social expenditure totalled 116.6 billion euros, while expenditure on minimum security/social assistance and refugee assistance by the Länder/municipalities amounted to only 1.6 billion euros (Statistics Austria 2021b).

the general public to finance those who cheat their way through the AMS [= Public Employment Service] with excuses" (as cited in Peternel/Bachner 2018). These statements were used to justify cuts and prepare stricter regulations (see above). The Austrian Public Employment Service, names "AMS", had increased sanctions against the unemployed by about 45% between 2016 and 2019 (Kopf 2020, as cited in Atzmüller/Knecht/Bodenstein 2020: 542). In its government programme, the coalition had already set out to "improve the effectiveness of sanctions" (ÖVP and FPÖ 2017, cf. Atzüller et al. (ÖVP/FPÖ 2017: 143f.). As part of the campaign against "cheating", there was also the discussion – in an amalgamation of insurance benefits and social transfers – about more far-reaching cuts such as the crediting of assets in unemployment assistance (Stelzer-Orthofer/Tamesberger 2018: 25; For the scenarios: Badelt et al. 2019). On the occasion of the presentation of the first nationwide social assistance basic law, Chancellor Kurz then directly linked the discussion about the lack of willingness to integrate and the abuse by asylum seekers with the justification for the new regulation of the minimum income: "Those who show 'unwillingness' to learn the German language, or cannot or do not want to work, will receive less money." (as cited in Die Presse 2018d).

Following these statements, the minimum income was reduced overall, the scope of the federal provinces for higher payments was eliminated, the amounts were strongly graded according to the number of children and – since unequal treatment of recognised refugees is not permitted under EU law – the amount was made dependent on the length of stay and language skills (Basic Social Assistance Act; in German: Sozialhilfegrundsatzgesetz); see also Atzmüller/Knecht/Bodenstein 2020). By reintroducing the former term of this benefit – "social assistance" – the objectives of the new law represented a remarkable departure from the provisions of the agreement between the federal level and the provinces, which had come into force in 2010 (Austrian National Assembly 2010) and which was dissolved in 2016. The 2010 agreement had stated that the aim of the federal government and the Länder was to "prevent poverty and social exclusion", to "intensify the fight against poverty and social exclusion" and to support people through sustainable reintegration into employment (see also Atzmüller/Knecht/Bodenstein 2020). In contrast, the new law (Austrian National Assembly 2020a) aimed to support only the general subsistence and accommodation of beneficiaries and their integration into work, without referring to poverty. In fact, the text of the law states that social assistance benefits should "take into account integration policy and alien police objectives" (Sozialhilfe-Grundsatzgesetz, §1). This legal regulation links the social provision of immigrants, but also of the Austrian population, with a supposed security policy (Atzmüller/Knecht/Bodenstein 2020). The commentary on the law makes it clear that the new law aims to reduce immigration by minimising the supposed pull factor of social assistance (Austrian National Assembly 2019). However, parts of the law were declared inadmissible by the Constitutional Court (Verfassungsgerichtshof 2019).

While the discourse on the introduction of compulsory training and education argued in favour of social investment and tended to conceal the coercive nature of the measure, the discussion on the reform of social assistance showed how a delegitimising discourse served to prepare cuts that had and still have far-reaching effects on the financial resources of those affected. The vagueness of the discredited and discriminated groups was strategically used to repeatedly position different population groups against each other (Knecht 2018). In fact, underage recipients of minimum benefits were and still are also affected by the cuts – their benefits were reduced to considerable extent. Underage recipients of benefits are in any case affected by poverty or are at risk of poverty in the sense of the EU-SILC statistics. In contrast to Germany (Freier 2015: 100f; Karl/ Schröder 2021) youths and young adults as minimum income recipients are hardly a public issue in Austria. Nevertheless, the (stirred up) sentiment against recipients of social benefits has been used to cut financial benefits within the framework of minimum security as well as other benefits of young people – as will be shown in the following (see chapter 4.3).

3.3 The discourses of experts and professionals and their political significance

In the course of carrying out the projects on which this paper is based, we examined not only public discourses but also, in particular, the discourses of experts and professionals who – bottom-up – have an impact on the political processes. For the SocIEtY project, for example, we conducted interviews at different levels of social service delivery. Among them were interview partners who work with young people in social institutions or in administration, but also senior staff of ministries (Knecht/Kuchler/Atzmüller 2014). The analysis of the interviews has been presented in various articles and discussed in different contexts (Knecht/Atzmüller 2019; Atzmüller/Knecht 2018; Knecht/Atzmüller 2017; Atzmüller/Knecht 2017a; Knecht 2016; Atzmüller/Knecht 2016a; Knecht 2014). The study shows that at the different levels of the political processes – in addition to shared convictions – different rationalities can be identified and are at work. In the following explanations, the focus is on the differences and commonalities of the statements of the following groups: firstly, the group of professionals who work with young people, secondly, the group of employees in the ministries and thirdly, the employers' representatives.

The discourse of the professionals in the field is essentially shaped by the discourse of their professional disciplines. Nevertheless, stereotypical ideas are sometimes put forward in the statements, as they are also taken up in the context of public discourses on the misuse of social benefits (see for quotes e.g. Knecht 2016: 854 and Knecht/Atzmüller 2017: 247; see also Ludwig-Mayerhofer/Behrend/Sondermann 2009). In an amalgamation of everyday discourses and professional discourses, our research simultaneously shows a frequent thematization of mental problems and illnesses. The young people were seen as increasingly deficient, lacking motivation and coming from dysfunctional families, discriminated against and pathologized (Atzmüller/Knecht 2017a; s. a. Preite 2019; Dahmen/Bonvin/Beuret 2017). In the process, a broad spectrum of mental illnesses was spoken of. However, the diffuse "diagnoses" of psychopathologies remained on their own; psychological or medical help was hardly addressed in the context. When asked about the problem of psychological problems, one of the youth coaches interviewed did not even declare himself responsible for the group of young people with mental illnesses (although psychological problems were repeatedly mentioned as a reason for the introduction of Youth Coaching (e.g. Bacher et al. 2014; Steiner/Pessl/Karaszek 2015) and saw the responsibilities as lying solely with health care facilities (AG Jugendcoaching 2018: 48). However, there is a lack of therapy places in the health care system, so that the young people cannot be helped (promptly) (see below).

Poverty, marginalisation and discrimination were not seen as the real problems of the young people, neither by the experts in the administration and the ministries nor by the professionals; neither was much attention paid to a system that wants to accelerate and strongly channel the career choice and that demands a lot from the young people in the process. It was also not a question of whether the members of the families of origin of those young people who were threatened with marginalisation had only a low level of formal education themselves. Rather, it was a question of the extent to which the families cared about the education and labour market options of the young people (Knecht/Atzmüller 2017: 245). The problems of young people therefore appeared less as a result of difficult socio-economic conditions, but were interwoven with a moralising view of (lower class) families. Against this background, measures for the reintegration of young people became therapeutic or therapy-substituting "compensation" for the lack of accompaniment and support by parents in coping with the transition from school to training and work (ibid.).

Discrimination to which young people were subject, among other things, because of attending a certain type of school or because of their migration history was mentioned, but its significance for the young people was considered to be low (Knecht/Kuchler/Atzmüller 2014; AG Jugendforschung 2018). The same was true for racist abuse that young people told professionals about and which was then left uncommented or partly downplayed (AG Jugendforschung 2018). In the interviews with experts, bullying among pupils was the most common topic, but hardly any problems with teachers, colleagues or superiors were mentioned (Knecht/Atzmüller 2019: 226). In fact, disadvantaged young people often have difficulties at school and in finding apprenticeships because of prejudice and discrimination (see also IDB 2016: 1). (s. a. IDB 2016–2019; Reckinger 2010; s. a. Knecht/Bodenstein 2019: 218). In interviews, youth coaches also reported discrimination by companies they were in contact with for the placement of apprenticeships (AG Jugendforschung 2018). The young people concerned are discriminated against at school because of the low level of education of their parents, because of their migration background or a non-Austrian citizenship (IDB 2016–2019); they are as well discriminated during their first steps on the training and labour market, where they may learn to "take" or "swallow" these experiences. However, professionals hardly use these discriminations to explain or relativize the difficulties or the failure of the young people (for example on the training market) or even to involve the parents more. Overall, the attitude of wanting to "go easy" on the young people became clear, instead of confronting them with their own social position and the processes through which they were or are disadvantaged (Knecht 2014: 231). In the interviews of the SocIEtY project, only once did a staff member of an institution that had explicitly made it its mission to support a strongly discriminated minority describe and recommend a different approach: In connection with a story about discrimination by a "right-wing extremist teacher", against which the pupils defended themselves by laughing at this person, she pleaded for educating the young people about their rights and possibilities to complain (ibid.).

As far as the justification of the measures is concerned, it became apparent during our interviews that most experts developed a superficial understanding for the young people and advocated pedagogical measures to compensate for the alleged lack of psychological/mental resources, their psychological problems as well as for their deficits in formal education and secondary virtues. Rather, the young people were supposed to learn "how to want e.g. a job" within the framework of these interventions. The pathologizing attributions functioned as the basis and legitimising strategy for pedagogical and activating measures such as compulsory training (Atzmüller/Knecht 2017a: 126) which was supposed to serve the "post-maturation" of the young people, according to a frequently used metaphor. The behaviour of the young people appeared to many professionals, probably against the background of the demands of the labour market, to be inadequate and not age-appropriate, but achievable by pedagogical means. The young people were to become "reasonable", whereby reasonableness was primarily defined as acceptance of the requirements and opportunities prevailing on the labour market (ibid.). In a view narrowed to employability, accepting an apprenticeship as soon as possible was usually seen as the most important goal (Knecht/Atzmüller 2017: 246). However, in the context of Youth Coaching, extended school careers also seem to be increasingly considered as a possible solution strategy.

In the statements of the ministries, the reduced view of job placement became even clearer through the terminology used, such as "get them into an apprenticeship" or "channel them into an internship" (as cited in Atzmüller/Knecht 2016a: 123). These terms make it clear that the inclusion of young people and their needs was seen here – compared to the goal of "placing" them in the labour market – only as a problem of peripheral interest. Accordingly, young women who did not continue their education after school, e.g. have children, were described as people who are "not in any system" or as "girls who disappear from the scene" (as cited in Knecht/Atzmüller 2017: 244). One ministry official attributed the function of pedagogical accompaniment in the context of Youth Coaching to "organising the young person in the best possible way" (as cited in Knecht 2014: 228).

The incapacitating and activating practice also influences the relationship between politics and social work (see also chapter 6). Although social work has been perceived by politicians and in the ministries as an independent discipline with independent goals (ebd; Knecht/Atzmüller 2017: 248), there have been attempts from various sides to oblige open youth work in particular to focus more strongly on the requirements of the training and labour market and to prepare young people accordingly (Knecht 2014: 230). Thus, in a brochure of the *Federal Network of Open Youth Work,* the minister responsible at the time called for "the prevention area to be expanded even further by extending offers [...]. Here I am thinking above all of targeted support offers for entering the labour market" (Federal Minister Mitterlehner in BOJA 2011, as cited in ibid.: 229). However, this orientation towards the labour market is an irritation for party-based open youth work, which sees itself on the side of young people and wants to work on their development and empowerment (Atzmüller/Knecht 2017a: 128; Oehme/Beran/Krisch 2007).

In some interviews with experts who were at the centre of the political process, the need for more measures and especially for the introduction of compulsory education (in the run-up to its introduction in 2017/2018) was justified in a different way. Here it was argued that only compulsory training would ensure in the long run that offers for young people would be made available in the political process at all (Knecht 2014: 228). What was not mentioned was the concern that measures could be reversed once the business of government was passed on. The introduction of the obligation was associated with the hope that a reversal would not be easy due to the higher binding force. In this kind of argumentation, the life situation and interests of the young people themselves played a subordinate role; instead, the mechanisms of the help system were in the foreground. This was also true for the hope expressed by youth coaches that compulsory education would finally lead to better cooperation between the schools which were to act as intermediaries to contact pupils (Knecht/Atzmüller 2019: 227). And indeed, a new situation seemed to arise for the schools, especially because they now had a role in the reporting system of dropouts. In the end, the ministry also confirmed that the compulsory training had decisively improved cooperation in the area of "school, training, youth work and the labour market".[28]

Employers' representatives, however, were generally sceptical about youth employment promotion measures because they focused too much on the needs of young people (Atzmüller/Knecht 2018). In this context, measures such as Supra-Company Training (SCT)[29] were also seen as effeminate "cuddly pedagogy" (ibid.: 8). For example, an employee of an employer organisation responsible for apprenticeship training considered apprenticeships in Supra-Company Training to be easier to complete (ibid.) and alledged that apprentices there had more holidays (SocIEtY project interview, as cited in Knecht/Kuchler/Atzmüller 2014: 509), which was not the case. Such attitudes, which are in line with the discourse of welfare abuse, can undermine meritocratic notions of justice (Atzmüller/Knecht 2017a) and legitimise cuts or the abolition of measures by pretending that young people only need to be activated more in order to get training places, apprenticeships and jobs.

Overall, it is evident that pathologizing interpretations and assessments by professionals underestimate the experiences and burdens (experiences of poverty, discrimination) of young people and – also against the background of social investment arguments – lead to the recommendation of incapacitating and guiding measures. In the statements of the professionals, the experts in the administrations and the employers' representatives, neither the explicit nor the implicit orientation towards concepts such as increasing the scope of action in the sense of Sen's capabilities, nor concepts of empowerment or greater political participation were of importance. The youngsters were not (yet) considered capable of making meaningful use of freedom of choice – or this aspiration was not even seen against the backdrop of fighting the shortage of skilled workers and forcing the channelling of young people into areas where a shortage could arise.

3.4 Discourses of professionals working in the field and subjectification by young people

Professional and public discourses, such as the discourses of legitimacy and justice, also play an important role at the meso and micro levels, for example

---

28 "*Training up to 18* has made a decisive contribution to improving cooperation in the area of schools, training, youth work and the labour market and, through its operational implementation with committees in which all relevant stakeholders participate, offers ideal-typical conditions for success-promoting cooperation." BMSGPK 2019 and SMS 2019 with reference to the study öibf/IHS 2019.
29 In German: "Überbetriebliche Lehrausbildung" = ÜBA.

in the provision of personal social services (such as counselling). The finding of our research that even professionals who deal with young people on a daily basis sometimes refer to simplistic and discriminatory discourses (e.g. about welfare recipients and people experiencing poverty) is also confirmed by studies in related fields.[30]

As already mentioned, the arguments of the professionals in the field differ from those of the experts in the administration. Regarding the behaviour of young people, experts in the administration more often problematised the lack of motivation of young people – a perspective that is also partly reflected in the public and the mass media. However, the professionals on site, i.e. social educators, social workers, youth workers or youth coaches, who are in contact with the young people, rather saw a problem in the fact that the young people had not learned to perceive themselves as self-effective (Knecht/Atzmüller 2017: 244). One of the interviewees also formulated the deficits in the context of a resource perspective: "But what has a much stronger impact beyond that is simply the lack of resources, that is, not only material resources, but also personal resources. [...] It starts with things like self-confidence or experiences of self-efficacy." (Interview of the SocIEtY project, as cited in Atzmüller/Knecht 2017a: 131).

Nevertheless, the view of many professionals regarding the young people is usually not resource-oriented, but deficit-oriented which limits the young people's opportunities instead of opening up perspectives. This can be an obstacle e.g. in counselling (Knecht 2016). Thus, in an interview of the SocIEtY project (see above, fn. 9), a woman who has since become a recognised artist said how she had been advised at school not to change to a grammar school. If the young people – contrary to the prejudices against them – express too ambitious career aspirations, teachers sometimes try to "cool down" their aspirations in career counselling or Youth Coaching.[31, 32]

The reaction of disadvantaged young people to the reservations they are confronted with usually consists in at least superficial adaptation to the demands and in silent resistance – and only rarely in learning to articulate and assert their needs or to rebel (Knecht/Atzmüller 2019; Atzmüller/Knecht

---

30 See for Germany Wiezorek/Pardo-Puhlmann 2013; Simon/Lochner/Prigge 2019; Kerle 2021.
31 See for Austria: Rothmüller 2014; for Germany: Walther/Walter/Pohl 2007, Knecht 2010: 186; for Switzerland: Preite 2021, 2022; on the concept of "cooling out" see Goffman 1952.
32 In the emancipatory terminology of social pedagogy, this was formulated by a ministry in a brochure on child and youth work: Child and youth work "is oriented [...] first and foremost towards their interests and needs. At the same time, it claims to empower these young people to self-determination and to motivate them to help shape society. By discovering their own abilities, but also their own limits, they have the chance to develop their own perspectives on life" (BMWFJ 2013: 6, as cited in Knecht/Atzmüller 2017: 248).

2017a). In a group interview, young people in a youth centre advocated the introduction of compulsory education with reference to possible misuse of social benefits and offers (AG Jugendforschung 2018) – and thus distinguished themselves from fictitious people whose position os similar to theirs, but who they fear are unwilling to commit to training and their future. They are the ones who need support, who are under the greatest pressure to justify themselves – and therefore sometimes also adopt pejorative attitudes towards imagined others ("othering") (s. a. Patrick 2016).

3.5 Results of the discourse analysis

It was shown how the pathologizing discourses about the allegedly deficient young people were used as a legitimising strategy for compulsory education (in the sense of an activating measure), while material poverty, marginalisation and discrimination of the young people hardly played a role in the argumentations. Taking of measures is legitimised within the framework of a social investment strategy that leads to more expenditure – "investment". In the area of social assistance, where the distrust of recipients of social benefits, which is fomented in public discourses, is in the foreground, the discourses also legitimise more activating measures (such as sanctions), but these go hand in hand with benefit cuts, because the social investment idea is not very present here.

In the more differentiated professional discourses, a more sympathetic picture of young people is ostensibly drawn, which is, however, also characterised by a paternalistic view: a lack of self-efficacy and motivation would lead to "post-maturation". (Knecht/Kuchler/Atzmüller 2014: 530) of the young people. This is not an attempt to initiate emancipatory processes, but above all to increase labour market orientation. The discourses serve to legitimise measures, such as the introduction of compulsory education, and thus ultimately have an impact on the way in which employment support for disadvantaged young people is organised and how resources are allocated.

Professionals dealing with adolescents also partly replicate the discourses about the misuse of social services and deficit families. Just as the pathologizing discourses do not lead to more psychotherapy for young people, the arguments about deficit families do not lead to more parental work; these arguments rather stabilise the legitimisation and application of activating measures. In the professional contact with young people, however, deficit-oriented views can limit their opportunities and stand in the way of their integration and success.

Although the discourses provide a direction for the (further) development of measures, the measures cannot be derived directly from them. Patterns of legitimisation, such as the discourse on the abuse of social benefits, shape the public discourse, e.g. in newspapers, in press releases or in the media. Nevertheless, there are degrees of freedom in implementation, which is why for a complex understanding of the transformation of the welfare state, legislation and the de facto implementation of measures must also be considered in the context of an institutional analysis.

4 Institutional changes of youth employment support in the government coalitions in Austria (2000–2020)

When the situation of young people on the labour market deteriorated in Austria in the 1980s, they became the subject of labour market policy for the first time in the post-war period (Melinz 1986; Knecht/Atzmüller 2019). At that time, attempts were made to create the supply of training places through new projects within the framework of a so-called "experimental labour market policy" (Lassnigg 1999: 9). Between 1986 and 1995 there was a higher supply of apprenticeship places than apprenticeship seekers in Austria (ibid.: 11). However, the shortage of apprenticeship places came to a head again at the end of the 1990s. Many of today's problems became more apparent for the first time at that time (cf. Lassnigg 2016: 38; Knecht/Preite 2022).

The measures of 1998 can be seen as the starting point of a "vocational support for disadvantaged persons" (Niedermair 2017) in Austria. Within this framework, two approaches were applied, both of which were further developed in the course of time: In the framework of the Youth Training Security Act[33] passed in 1998 (Republic of Austria 1998), extra-company offers were developed for young people who could not find an apprenticeship place or had dropped out of an apprenticeship (Knecht/Atzmüller 2019). In the first cohort, around 4,200 young people held so-called JASG apprenticeship places; later (2006/07) there were already 11,200 individuals (Schneeberger 2009: 65). In addition, in 1998 a tax-reducing "apprenticeship allowance"[34] was introduced amounting to 20,000 Schilling (approx. 1,450 €) per year for each apprentice of a company (Austrian National Assembly 1998; Dornmayr/Löffler 2020). Nevertheless, the number of apprenticeship places decreased and has been decreasing in the long-term trend (see Tab. 1).

The following sub-chapters (4.1 to 4.3) present the institutional development of the three government coalitions in the period 2000 to 2020 in order to be able to describe the respective social policy impetus. Within this period there were two coalitions of the christian-conservative ÖVP with the populist far-right FPÖ (2000–2007 and 2017–2020) and a "grand coalition" of the social-democratic SPÖ with the ÖVP lasting from 2007 to 2017.

---

33 Jugendausbildungs-Sicherungsgesetz, JASG.
34 § 124b Z 31 EstG.

4.1 ÖVP-FPÖ-Coalition I (2000–2007): The expansion of the company-oriented apprenticeship promotion

The first coalition of the christian-conservative ÖVP with the far-right FPÖ (2000-2007) is commonly dubbed *Black-Blue I* (in German: "schwarz-blau I") (Lehner/ Wodak 2020: 179). From the economic crisis of 2002 onwards, the coalition had to struggle with rising unemployment figures. Due to inner-party tensions resulting from the participation in the government, the party split zup, a move that was initiated by Jörg Haider. From 2005 onwards, the ÖVP governed with the new Haider party Bündnis *Zukunft Österreich* (BZÖ), which chose the colour orange for itself, which is why it is also referred to as "Black-Blue/Orange". However, since there was continuity in terms of personnel, in the following we will speak of "Black-Blue I" for the sake of simplicity, although the aforementioned government period formally comprised two different coalitions.

According to the government programme of 2000, further development of apprenticeship training was to be achieved, among other things, by reforming the vocational training law – for example, by developing new apprenticeship occupations and modernising existing ones, by "specific training offers for young people with learning deficits" (Austrian Government 2000: 79f.) and the introduction of training associations (ibid.). At the same time, training was to be made "practical and unbureaucratic", among other things by "combing through protective provisions for factual justification and proportionality" (ibid.: 79), furthermore by extending the probationary period to three months and by allowing daytime training until 11 pm. The ratio of apprentices to skilled workers that could be employed was to be relaxed as well (ibid.).

The main changes, however, consisted in the subsidisation of training companies. The tax-reducing "apprenticeship allowance" that existed between 1998 and 2002 was replaced by a more lavish apprenticeship training premium (2002–2008, § 108f EStG) of € 1,000 to € 2,000 per apprentice and apprenticeship year, which was financed through social security contributions (Dornmayr/Litschel/Löffler 2016: 16). This benefit was supplemented by the so-called Blum bonus (2005–2008). This bonus, which amounted to € 4,800 in the first apprenticeship year, € 2,400 in the second apprenticeship year and € 1,200 in the third apprenticeship year, was granted to those companies that created new apprenticeship positions and was thus the first subsidy that was linked to a condition. However, the Blum bonus – like the apprenticeship subsidy as a whole later on – was criticised for high deadweight effects. (Wacker 2007; BMASK 2013a: 254f; cf. also Dornmayr/Nowak 2019: 48; OECD 2019, chapter 2). The subsidy was also used by companies that would have trained apprentices in any case. An evaluation commissioned by the AMS nevertheless praises this type of subsidy, as it "also [has] a compensatory effect on the company side, in that companies with a weaker training organisation and greater training difficulties tend to be subsidised disproportionately often" (Dornmayr/Litschel/Löffler 2017: 2). This would promote companies "which are themselves disadvantaged in the competition for the most talented young people and therefore come into contact more frequently with 'lower-performing' applicants and/or apprentices" (ibid.). This shows to what extend the promotion of apprenticeships was understood in the sense of a business-friendly economic policy – and not in the sense of a labour market policy or policy for young people (s. a. FPÖ Bildungsinstitut n.y. [2011]: 197).

Enterprises employing apprentices were also favoured in other respects, e.g. through a reduction of the employer/employee share in health insurance and continued payment of wages (Obinger/Tálos 2006: 114; Schmid n.d.), through an exemption from all contributions to accident insurance[35] (at the expense of taxpayers) and through further regulations of the comprehensive Budget Accompanying Act 2003 (Republic of Austria 2003; s. a. Obinger/Tálos 2006: 114). In addition, the new government extended the permission for night work for apprentices in the catering industry from 10 p.m. to 11 p.m. in the first weeks after taking office. (Bonvalot 2017: 49; Republic of Austria 2000: 811). As announced, the probationary period for apprentices was also extended from two to three months. (Obinger/Tálos 2006: 132) and the termination of apprenticeship contracts was simplified (§15 Vocational Training Act, Schmid n.d.). In cooperation with the Economic Chamber and the Public Employment Service (AMS), job placement projects with a focus on specific sectors were launched. (Obinger/Tálos 2006: 133).

Overall, it can be seen that the labour force of apprentices was "flexibilised" by restricting workers' rights in the first Black-Blue government period. Many of the measures point to their original idea: Although there were enough apprenticeship places, they were not "called upon" by young people or it was not interesting for companies to hire apprentices because of the cost structure. The general labour market policy of this government period took an even more activating direction and was oriented towards company interests. Thus combi-wage models were used, which enabled employers to hire employees below the usual wage costs. (ibid.). Similar to the subsidy of apprenticeships, combi-wage models are based on the argument that hiring employees would not be profitable due to too high wages or too high wage demands and therefore the wage costs for the company side would have to be reduced through subsidies. However, such arguments negate, for example, the emergence of the apprenticeship gap through the reduction of apprenticeships due to structural change.

During the Black-Blue-I Coalition, a reform of the provisions of the asylum law also affected young people as well as adults: At the turn of the millennium, the current legal situation still stated that asylum seekers could take up employ-

---

35 General Social Security Act, §51, para. 6, amended by the Budgetbegleitgesetz 2003 (Republic of Austria 2003).

ment three months after filing an asylum application (Langthaler 2019). In 2004, however, this right was restricted by the so-called *Bartenstein Decree* – named after the then Minister of Economics and Labour Martin Bartenstein. The decree stipulated that asylum seekers – as long as their case has not been decided – may only work for a limited period of time, i.g. for a maximum of six months per year and only in the fields of agriculture and tourism. Quotas were set annually for each province and sector (§5 AuslBG). Only within the framework of these quotas could asylum seekers receive a work permit. However, it was problematic to return to the basic benefits for asylum seekers after a job, so accepting these jobs was a risk. Only in the case of recognition were asylum seekers at least formally equal to nationals, although even then they were confronted with discrimination and stigmatisation. The regulations of the *Bartenstein Decree* were repealed in July 2021, as the Constitutional Court concluded that the decree was unlawful.[36] The long duration of the decree being applied shows what far-reaching effects unlawful decrees and laws can have.

Thus, the policy of promoting youth employment can best be understood as a "patronage policy" in favour of entrepreneurs than as a pure neoliberal market policy. This is shown by the high importance of subsidies ("Förderungen") in the area of apprenticeship employment. The exclusion of asylum-seeking youth from the labour market is also a measure that does not correspond to (neo-)liberal principles. In its exclusionary nature, it corresponds to the character of a racist-legitimised right-wing populist/extreme right policy of exclusion (see below).

4.2 SPÖ-ÖVP-Coalition (2007–2017): From the training guarantee to compulsory training

The beginning of the grand coalition of SPÖ and ÖVP of the years 2007 to 2017 was also marked by a financial and economic crisis and its consequences. The number of in-company apprenticeship places had decreased almost continuously in the previous 20 years, for example in the period from 2007 to 2017 from 126,831 to 97,512, i.e. by 23%. The number of companies providing training fell from 38,132 to 27,792, i.e. by 27%. (Dornmayr/Nowak 2019: 12 and 38).

Against this background, the training guarantee was introduced in 2008, guaranteeing school leavers and unemployed young people the possibility to

---

36 Szigetvari 2021; Verfassungsgerichtshof 2021. The current government then hastened to state that in practice it wanted to leave everything as it was. See Der Standard 2021; Graber/Widmann 2021.

complete an apprenticeship in a supra-company training workshop if no apprenticeship position is found in a company (Knecht/Atzmüller 2019). This guarantee had already been demanded by the SPÖ in parliament in 2002 (Austrian National Assembly 2002: 112). This Supra-Company Training (SCT) partly takes place in apprenticeship workshops, partly it is organised in the form of several internships. It formally leads to a regular apprenticeship qualification. It is possible to switch from SCT to an in-company apprenticeship at any time – an option that is frequently taken up (Hofbauer/Kugi-Mazza/Sinowatz 2014). However, the remuneration in the SCT is lower than in a company-based apprenticeship. In Austria, 10% of apprenticeships are already offered as supra-company apprenticeships – there is even talk of a new pillar of vocational education and training (Schlögl et al. 2020). Within the framework of the training guarantee and in preparation for the introduction of the apprenticeship/training obligation, the fragmented project landscape has been unified since 2012 into a support system with three pillars (s. a. Knecht/Preite 2022: 130):

- The first pillar of this is the *Supra-Company Training* presented above.
- The second pillar, *Youth Coaching,* is a nationwide counselling programme for young people who are about to finish compulsory schooling (normally at 15) and are uncertain about their career choice. In order to prevent them from dropping out of the education and training "system", they are advised mostly at school by external youth coaches (Knecht 2016).
- Under the term *AusbildungsFit ("Fit for Vocational Training")* – formerly or in the meantime called *production schools* – various training measures for young people who are not considered ready for apprenticeship training were summarised. (cf. Atzmüller/Knecht 2016a). Previously – formulated in sporting metaphor – *AusbildungsFit* was already responsible for "school-weary"[37] young people. The Ministry sees the goal of this measure "in stabilising, increasing motivation, imparting technical knowledge and basic qualification" (BMASK 2015b: 93; cf. Fasching 2019).

Within this framework, not only the strongly growing funds for the employment promotion of young people can be understood despite restrained budgetary policy – since 2000, this area has been promoted with ever higher sums and institutionally expanded (2001: € 168.8 million, 2008: € 561.8 million 2019: € 925.9 million; see Tab. 3, col. 1). There is also the tendency of employment promotion to instrumentalise or colonise classic open youth work (Knecht 2014). In networked cooperation, institutions of open youth work are seen as "suppliers" or they are asked to offer job application training for the young people (see also chapter 1). Both the SCT and in the Ausbildungsfit offers comprise social pedagogical support; the Youth Coaching staff members

---

37 BMAS 2013, as cited in Knecht 2014: 226.

belong to different social professions. In addition, coordination offices were set up at the state and federal level to create an overview of the offers in transition and coordinate them (Knecht 2016: 226).

The promotion of apprenticeships was reformed in several steps in 2008. Attempts were made to ensure the promotion was based on qualitative criteria. In this way, the quality of training was to be increased and the situation of disadvantaged groups of apprentices was to be improved (Dornmayr/Petanovitsch/Winkler 2016: 19f.): For example, apprenticeship training for adults and in-company training for apprentices coming from a Supra-Company-Training institution were promoted, as were young people who were disadvantaged on the labour market due to "disabilities", "social problems" or "school deficits", as well as girls in apprenticeship occupations with a low proportion of women (ibid.; cf. also below, chapter 6.3).

With a long lead time, the training guarantee was transformed into a training obligation effective from autumn 2017[38], and was – as already mentioned above – introduced under the euphemistic name "Training up to 18"[39] (Atzmüller/Knecht 2016a; Schlögl 2016) and complements the existing training guarantee. Since then, school leavers or school dropouts under 18 can no longer change to unskilled or semi-skilled employment, but must start an apprenticeship or a measure with the Austrian Public Employment Service *AMS*. If the regulations on compulsory education are violated, parents are fined between €100 and €1,000. The government justified the introduction of compulsory training by saying that this measure would serve to secure growth and employment, that the unemployment rate of unskilled workers was very high and that "we cannot and do not want to afford a 'lost generation'" (BMASK, n.d., as cited in Knecht/Atzmüller 2019: 221).

In the context of the compulsory training, the already existing monitoring system of Youth Coaching MBI[40], which had already collected a lot of data, some of it very personal,[41] from the young people (Knecht 2014: 233), was supplemented by another monitoring system MAB[42] in order to bring together the information of all parties required to report (including schools, parents and apprenticeship places) and to identify young people who "drop out of the system" (Gesslbauer et al.: 5) – a popular expression in professional discourse[43] – to filter them out. Coordination offices were introduced specifically to monitor compulsory training.

---

38   Republic of Austria 2016 (Training Obligations Act = Ausbildungspflichtgesetz – APflG).
39   In German: "AusBildung bis 18".
40   Monitoring Berufliche Integration – MBI.
41   Among other things, also a special educational need identified by the school or information about personal problems.
42   Monitoring AusBildung bis 18 – MAB.
43   Bissuti et al. 2013: 92, Gučanin 2013, BMASK 2013b: 29.

The data collected is to be used, among other things, to examine the efficiency of measures; an "education-related employment career monitoring" had already been installed previously (cf. BMASK 2020: 17). Thus, the monitoring and recording of education and training trajectories is being advanced, which should serve the further development of the transition system. The increasing monitoring, controlling and steering of education and career paths reflect both the revaluation of education as a resource and the narrowed view of employability and the accentuation of the human capital aspect of education. However, studies that focus on the subjectivity of young people or even the subjective meaning of education are rare (cf. Sting/Knecht 2022).

Both the training guarantee introduced in 2008 and the compulsory training introduced in 2017 do not apply to young asylum seekers who are in the asylum procedure, although this was demanded several times in the legislative process (see e.g. Dornmayr/Wieser 2010: 108 and Schatz 2017). The Red-Black Government also failed to comply with repeated motions calling for the lifting of the quasi-work ban for all asylum seekers, which dates back to the Black-Blue-I Government (e.g. Alev Korun, Austrian National Assembly 2013: 71), although since 2013 there has been a binding EU directive that stipulates that asylum seekers must have access to the labour market no later than nine months after filing their application, even if the asylum application has not yet been decided.[44] For young asylum seekers, this means that their lives are marked by pointless waiting (Bodenstein/Knecht 2017; Sting/Knecht 2022). Asylum procedures often drag on for a long time[45] (Bodenstein/Knecht 2017). The fact that since 2016 the asylum granted has been limited for the first three years ("asylum for a limited period"; in German: "Asyl auf Zeit"; Austrian National Assembly 2016), tends to aggravate the situation (Kurier 2016a; Bonavida 2018).

However, in a weakening of the *Bartenstein Decree* (see above), the possibility to complete an apprenticeship in so-called shortage occupations ("Mangelberufen"), i.e. in occupations in which apprenticeship positions could not be regularly filled, was created in two steps (in 2012 and 2015) for adolescents and young adults up to 25 (Knecht/Bodenstein 2019: 218; Langthaler 2019) – but companies had to prove in an elaborate manner that they could not find another Austrian applicant or applicant from an EU country for the apprenticeship and the Public Employment Service AMS had to confirm this (Knecht/Bodenstein 2019; Langthaler 2019). At the same time, young people were denied help from the labour market service in their job search (ibid.). Despite the

---

44 EU Reception Conditions Directive of 2013, Art. 15; European Parliament 2013, see also Szigetvari 2020.
45 "Asylum procedures took an average of 16.5 months in 2017, according to information from the Federal Office for Immigration and Asylum (BFA)" (Expertenrat für Integration 2018: 27). Otherwise, there is hardly any public data on this. The official maximum duration of procedures was increased from 6 to 15 months in 2016; however, there are also procedures that take several years.

high hurdles, apprenticeships in shortage occupations were attractive for young asylum seekers, as there were neither vocational nor general education offers for them after they had fulfilled their compulsory schooling – especially due to the exclusion from the training guarantee and obligation (Knecht/Bodenstein 2019; Knecht/Tamesberger 2019).

After the arrival of many asylum seekers in 2015, two further laws, that were intended to promote integration and also affected young people, were passed in 2017. The Integration Act was aimed at people whose stay in Austria is clarified in the asylum procedure. It combined the right to integration measures with the obligation to take advantage of them. The measures consisted, among other things, of German courses (up to level A2) combined with so called *value and orientation courses.* However, it became apparent that these course measures had little influence on labour market integration (Hosner/Vana/Khun Jush 2017) whereas studies comparing countries showed that arriving asylum seekers' long labour market absences permanently worsened their labour market chances (Marbach/Hainmueller/Hangartner 2018). Another measure, the integration year, obliges unemployed persons granted asylum and beneficiaries of subsidiary protection to participate and contribute to labour market support measures. It usually lasts one year and is a modular labour market promotion measure (from language level A1), which is partly completed in the form of community service. The discussion about the introduction of the laws was characterised, among other things, by the alleged unwillingness of asylum seekers to work and to integrate socially and culturally[46], which is why values and orientation courses were integrated into both measures.

Overall, for the Red-Black Coalition that lasted ten years was characterized on the one hand by a good supply situation for Austrian youths due to the training guarantee, but on the other hand also by an increasing obligation through the "Training until 18" within the framework of a social-investment model. As far as asylum seekers are concerned, the exclusionary line of the previous coalition was in principle maintained, but slightly more perspectives were opened up through access to apprenticeships in shortage occupations. By not including them in compulsory education and training, discrimination was again further exacerbated. The value and orientation courses, which were established against a racist background and which could have been subjectivised by the participants in the sense of othering, may also have had an exclusionary effect. However, there was no discussion about disturbed recognition processes (psychological/mental experience as a refugee, but also formal recognition of previous

---

46 On activation, see e.g. Austrian National Assembly 2017a: "The compulsory integration year is based on a system of support and demand. [...] The concrete integration offers are accompanied by the obligation to cooperate and the possibility of sanctioning in case of non-participation in offered measures."

work achievements), although these can impair the development of psychological/mental resources.

4.3 ÖVP-FPÖ-Coalition II (2017–2019): The activation of Austrian youths and the blocking of young asylum-seekers

The ÖVP-FPÖ coalition with Chancellor Sebastian Kurz (ÖVP) and Vice-Chancellor Heinz-Christian Strache (FPÖ) discussed cuts in social benefits soon after taking office in December 2017 (see above) – after the election campaign for the 2017 National Council elections, which was strongly marked by the so-called "long summer of migration" (from 2015 on) and its consequences. Although the Austrian People's Party ÖVP continued to govern in the new government as the now stronger coalition partner, a strong new influence by the far-right FPÖ was also felt in employment policy for young people. The FPÖ had already defined the line of its apprenticeship policy in its "Handbook" (FPÖ Bildungsinstitut n.y. [2011]) outlined. The following problems were seen there: "Managing motivation of young people, a poor image of the dual training 'apprenticeship' and the ever-increasing shortage of apprenticeship places" (ibid.: 198). These problems would lead to "in return, the economy demanding more and more workers from abroad" (ibid.). The FPÖ therefore wanted to increase the financial incentive to hire apprentices – a measure it also saw as an "effective form of economic promotion for our small and medium-sized enterprises" (ibid.: 200). At the same time, it advertised that this model "counteracts the trend that more and more apprentices are trained in less productive, protected areas outside the companies at the expense of their training quality" (ibid.: 200) – without seeing that their subsidies could, after all, also contribute to keeping companies with low productivity alive. Also, "excessive legal hurdles for ending the probationary period [...] should be removed" (ibid.: 200) with the aim of being able to deploy workers more flexibly.

In fact, the new coalition took various steps in this direction in its government programme (ÖVP/FPÖ 2017) and quickly tackled the implementation after taking office: The Supra-Company Training (SCT), which was perceived as an alternative offer to regular in-company apprenticeships, was particularly affected. In order to build more pressure on young people to accept regular apprenticeships instead of places in SCT, all apprentices in SCT were obliged to permanently apply for in-company apprenticeship places (Knecht/Bodenstein 2019: 218; Szigetvari 2018b). At the same time, the Public Employment Service AMS formulated higher mobility requirements for young people, as there were/are more vacant apprenticeship places in the west of Austria (especially in Tyrol and Vorarlberg) and more apprenticeship seekers in the east (especially in Vienna). In addition, the "training allowance" of Supra-Company Training, i.e. the remuneration of apprentices in the SCT, was reduced from € 753 to € 325 in the first two apprenticeship years (Knecht/Tamesberger 2019). In addition to the reduction of the young people's fees, the budget for the SCT was also reduced as part of general cuts in the AMS budget. Some of the providers had to close facilities (cf. ibid.). These measures were intended to build up pressure so that young people would be more likely to accept jobs in companies (ÖVP/FPÖ 2017: 145).

From the government's point of view, there were various reasons for this approach: On the one hand, the fact that there was and is a higher proportion of young people with migration experience among the participants could have played a role in the criticism of the SCT from the far right[47]; on the other hand, the SCT was criticised because it was expensive (for the state) compared to an in-company apprenticeship (Dornmayr/Nowak 2017: 112) and because – despite the general lack of apprenticeship places – applicants could not be found for all vacancies. In particular, unattractive apprenticeship positions in the catering industry (Reisenzaun 2016) and in tourism sometimes could not be filled (Knecht/Bodenstein 2019). Concerns were also voiced that young school leavers will not accept the allegedly comfortable situation or "cosy pedagogy" (Atzmüller/Knecht 2018: 8) in SCT facilities, where there were also socio-educational activities, and were likeliy to prefer the employment conditions in private companies (cf. Knecht/Kuchler/Atzmüller 2014: 509). These fears were surprising insofar as many young people assessed this type of apprenticeship as "second-class" anyway and the amounts previously paid out were already below the regular apprenticeship income[48] (ebd; Atzmüller/Knecht 2017b: 124). The procedure of the SCT was also changed: The apprentices were to be given the earliest and most sustainable placement possible through the obligatory involvement of companies in the design of the training and the daily training routine (Dornmayr/Löffler 2020: 4f.). For Stelzer-Orthofer and Tamesberger (2018) the impression arose "that the government perceives SCT in competition with in-company apprenticeship training, which concerns both the young people and the financial resources".

In order to promote in-company apprenticeships, the new Black-Blue ÖVP-FPÖ coalition – just like the first one – pushed ahead with the direct promotion of apprenticeships (BMDW 2018). It was already stated in the government programme that the promotion of enterprises should be further expanded

---

47 On the attitude of the FPÖ see e.g. FPÖ Bildungsinstitut n.y. [2011]: 197f.; on young people: Dornmayr/Löffler 2020: 142; see also Atzmüller/Knecht/Bodenstein 2020.
48 The apprentices' income was called "apprenticeship compensation" in Austria until 2019.

(ÖVP/FPÖ 2017). In fact, the "subsidy for the in-company training of apprentices" (§ 19c Vocational Training Act) was increased from € 162.8 million in 2017 (subsidy report 2017) to € 229.9 million in 2019 (subsidy report 2019)[49] (see Tab. 3). In addition, adolescents and young adults were also subject to the tightening of general labour market policy measures and labour law regulations: For example, apprentices of full age were affected by the amendment of the working hours regulation in the Working Hours and Rest Act, which made it possible for employees to work up to twelve hours a day (instead of ten as before) and up to 60 hours a week (instead of 48 hours as before).[50] Already in the government programme, in addition to a reform of the reasonableness provisions in job search, an "improvement of the effectiveness of sanctions" was demanded (ibid.: 143f.) in order to increase the pressure on the (long-term) unemployed in particular (Atzmüller/Knecht/Bodenstein 2020; Hammer 2018). Accordingly, sanctions against the unemployed increased by about 45% between 2016 and 2019 (Kopf 2020, as cited in Atzmüller/Knecht/Bodenstein 2020: 542; Theurl 2022).

The new government also took the lead in abolishing the Youth Council of Confidence and instead lowering the voting age for works council elections to 16. The Youth Council of Confidence has a similar function for underage employees in Austria as the works council for adults:[51] They are supposed to take care of the concerns of apprentices and young employees in the company. In addition, the institution of the youth council of confidence serves to practice co-determination in the company. It was not until 2010 that councils of confidence were also installed in Supra-Company Trainings (AMS Austria 2013: 9; BAG §30c). This institution should now be abolished. The third of apprentices who are younger than 16 would have completely lost the possibility of co-determination in the company. A draft law was dropped at the last minute due to trade union campaigns and parliamentary initiatives (Zaunbauer 2019).

The increased pressure and obligation to education and work that young people are exposed to is in paradoxical contrast to the limited access to education and work of asylum-seeking young people: In September 2018, the possibility for asylum seekers to do an apprenticeship in a shortage occupation was abolished. Prior to this change, an internal coalition discussion had risen about whether it was desirable that young asylum seekers were allowed to do an apprenticeship during the asylum procedure (Knecht/Bodenstein 2019). The regional Chambers of Commerce and even parts of the governing party ÖVP

---

49 This includes boarding costs for apprentices, which thus no longer have to be borne by the companies or apprentices.
50 §9 Abs 1 AZG; Republic of Austria 2018; Chamber of Labour Upper Austria 2018; Knecht/Tamesberger 2019.
51 § 128ff. Labour Constitution Act: Youth Councils of Confidence have campaigned for issues such as covering accommodation and travel costs when the vocational school is far away. In 2014 there were about 2,400 youth councils of confidence in Austrian companies (Knecht/Kuchler/Atzmüller 2014: 522).

opposed the government on this issue (Die Presse 2018b). Here the guiding principles of different parts of the government clashed and – similar to the discussions on the introduction of the 12-hour working day – the area of friction between a partly pro-business neo-liberal course and the populist exclusionary policy of the FPÖ, which has always liked to present itself as a "social home party" ("Soziale Heimatpartei"), became obvious (Knecht/Bodenstein 2019), whereby the exclusionary policies even prevailed against the majority opinion of the population (Der Standard 2018a). However, the share of asylum seekers in apprenticeships is very low: only 1,000 out of 106,000 apprentices are asylum seekers. It could therefore hardly be a matter of protecting apprenticeships for Austrian young people against asylum-seeking competition: Apprenticeships in shortage occupations are often not particularly attractive and therefore cannot be filled. The abolition of apprenticeships for asylum-seeking young people was probably primarily about using a *symbolic policy* (Edelman 2005) of exclusion (Knecht/Bodenstein 2019). Integration is thus likely to be prevented – and moreover it possibly was seen as advantageous that the process of deportation was simplified.[52] A discussion arose as to whether apprentices had to terminate their apprenticeship immediately or whether existing apprenticeship contracts could still be completed regularly. The government countered the criticism that integrated and hard-working asylum-seeking apprentices were being deported against the interests of employers by proposing an extension of access to the apprenticeship market for young third-country nationals[53] (Der Standard 2018b; Die Presse 2018c). This would have meant that the asylum-seeking young people would be replaced by young people from third countries who do not apply for asylum – and who, due to the way the *Red-White-Red Card* is constructed, would not be entitled to social benefits such as minimum security/social assistance or unemployment benefits.

The abolition of the possibility to do an apprenticeship in a shortage occupation was significant for young people seeking asylum because – as already noted above – these young people are no longer entitled to go to school or to be trained once they have fulfilled their compulsory training, i.e. at around the age of 15: Asylum-seeking young people are excluded from the education guarantee and the education obligation. At the same time, the government has reduced integration and education projects targeting this age group through massive cuts at the AMS (Knecht/Bodenstein 2019: 218). Under the protest of the welfare associations, the AMS funds for the integration of migrants and persons entitled to asylum were massively reduced (John 2018; Die Presse 2018d; Hagen 2018). This also affected measures within the framework of the

---

52 Deportations of young people and apprentices – in some cases directly from their place of work – have repeatedly caused and continue to cause expressions of solidarity and resistance among the population (e.g. Die Presse 2020).
53 Third-country nationals are people who come from countries that are not members of the EU.

Integration Year Act such as German courses, competence checks and vocational counselling – all measures that had been introduced only a short time before to enable integration and a successful entry into the labour market (Knecht/Tamesberger 2019). This also drew the attention of the Federal President Alexander Van der Bellen, who criticised the cuts: one could not "reduce the German courses, but then take German language skills into account with the money. That is clearly contradictory.", He also stated that integration should be pursued "in our own interest" (Die Presse 2018a).

Looking at the plans and implemented measures of the ÖVP-FPÖ Government (2017–2019) reveals that its policy style can be described as "business-friendly and paternalistic": The policy apparently only very partially pursued a neoliberal austerity policy, which included the reduction of social benefits. A restructuring rather than a dismantling of welfare state services took place (Atzmüller/Knecht/Bodenstein 2020; Atzmüller 2022). For example, funding for the SCT and for the apprentices working in it was cut. This put more pressure on young people in their search for apprenticeship places and during their apprenticeship; they were sometimes pushed into less attractive and unsuitable apprenticeship places. However, maintaining and expanding expensive subsidies for companies that take on apprentices is a strongly interventionist policy that contradicts a neoliberal policy style and is more typical of conservative ("state-dominated/corporative") welfare states.

The right-wing populist/extreme right policy of exclusion against asylum-seeking young people, which is described as "organised disintegration" (Täubig 2009), as "exclusion within inclusion" (Stichweh 1997) or as "administration of exclusion" (Bommes/Scherr 2000) impedes the integration of these young people and leads to precarious material living situations and greater psychological strain (Knecht/Bodenstein 2019). This exclusionary policy towards asylum-seeking youth (e.g. in the form of abolishing apprenticeships in shortage occupations and keeping them out of the labour market) is explicitly opposed to neoliberal principles that value a large supply of labour and brand the failure to use human capital resources as ineffective. It is consistent with the policies of conservative welfare states in that it tends to rectify the stratification of the society and to reduce social mobility.

The combination of the enforced measures ultimately leads to the situation, which at first glance seems contradictory, that more pressure is exerted on young people from Austria and other EU countries to accept an apprenticeship, to continue their education and to work, while at the same time young people seeking asylum are denied or prohibited from doing exactly this. This supposed contradiction can be explained by the fact that the interest in trained workers is in opposition to an interest in exclusion (of asylum seekers). Contrary to what is sometimes superficially portrayed in the media, it is not just about access to welfare state benefits, but about preventing integration through exclusion from the labour market.

5 Results and conclusions: On the governance of the welfare state

Chapter 5.1 summarises the results of the discourse analysis and the institutional analysis and shows the relationships to the different resources and the social policy guidelines. While chapter 5.2 then discusses social inequalities and tendencies towards division – also in the context of considerations of social justice – chapter 5.3 (deepening the topic of social inequality) discusses the way in which right-wing populist/extremely right policies distribute or allocate opportunities. Chapter 5.4 shows why the welfare state should not only be understood as an institution that distributes resources "from the top down" – and that it is therefore important to also consider the opposite direction "from the bottom up" in the analysis.

5.1 Results of discourse analysis and institutional analysis

If one asks, as does Amartya Sen, about the information basis of judgments of justice,[54] then – *with regard to the discourse analysis* – in the public discourses and the professional discourses about disadvantaged young people – the special importance of education in general and formal educational qualifications in particular becomes apparent. In the discussion, indicators such as "NEETs" and "early school leavers" (ESL) were important variables, whose development not only says something about the young people, but is equally influenced by the labour market situation and education policy. The fact that the rate of ESL was declining even without compulsory training/education was not relevant in the understanding of the problem in the field of employment promotion for disadvantaged youth.

Event the professionals made hardly any statements on material poverty and social inequality in the young people's life situations. As has been shown, assumptions about deficient parental homes and psychological/mental problems were used instead for the interpretation of the young people's situations, however, the clinical extent of which was hardly surveyed or taken for serious. In particular, a certain scepticism about the motivation and self-efficacy of the young people was revealed. Motivation and self-efficacy, like other psychological/mental resources, were primarily discussed as missing resources in the context of the young people's deficits. Motivation was understood more as a

---

54 "Informational basis of the judgement of justice" = IBJJ (Sen 1990); see also SocIEtY Consortium 2014, Knecht/Kuchler/Atzmüller 2014: 494f. and Atzmüller/Knecht 2017b.

stable trait rather than a resource that results from complex recognition relationships and personal contacts, but can also be limited by experienced or suffered discriminating attributions (Lehmkuhl/Schmidt/Schöler 2013; Wellgraf 2014) (see also chapter 6.3).

The *institutional analysis* showed that the policies of the different coalitions focus on different resources and can be clearly assigned to different guiding principles. Social investment policy focuses primarily on education as a resource, but also addresses mental resources. A neoliberal or corporate policy focuses primarily on the resource of money/income and on the associated incentive mechanisms. Right-wing populist/extreme right (social) policy uses discourses that exclude specific groups and thus implements policies that (further) block the use of socio-political as well as existing resources for these groups.

Looking at the different government periods, it is above all the *policy of the Red-Black Government of 2008–2017* that follows the guiding principle of the social investment state, even if this term is not used in public. Young people – and especially disadvantaged young people – are "invested" in: As mentioned, expenditure has increased from € 168.8 million in 2001 to € 561.8 million in 2008 and to € 933.0 million in 2018 (See Tab. 3, col. 1). As part of this policy, the establishment of inter-company training should reduce the depencance of acquiring education (and also the generation of initial income) on cyclical fluctuations in the supply of training places or their general decline in the long term. SCT is discussed as the beginning of a system change or as a separate pillar alongside apprenticeship and school education (Schlögl et al. 2020) and represents a sensible alternative to remaining stuck n preparatory qualification measures that do not lead to a vocational qualification.[55] However, this is a (vocational) education policy that primarily serves a labour market and socio-political purpose, as the measures are primarily aimed at averting training unemployment and subsequent unemployment –following an education concept that is reduced to "employability".

While the great extent and increase in stress among young people have been observed, these arguments have not – as might be expected – led to an expansion of the offer of psychotherapy places or other measures of pedagogical or psychological support, strengthening or resilience promotion (Plener et al. 2021; Fliedl/Ecker/Karwautz 2020; Philipp et al. 2018; Kienbacher 2018, 2017; Fuchs/Karwautz 2017; Fliedl 2013). In fact, there was (and still is) a considerable lack of care, especially in the field of psychotherapy (ibid.), but also in the field of school social work and school psychology.

As in other areas of social and labour market policy, this type of social investment policy – which is heavily dependent on the participation of those concerned – was increasingly obligatory and activating: this was particularly

---

55 Cf. on the situation in Germany: Enggruber/Fehlau (2018) – and on the situation in Switzerland: Knecht/Preite (2022).

evident in the transition from the training guarantee to the training obligation. access to the measures (as educational resources) was virtually conceived as a barter transaction (obligatory for the young people): The young people are obliged to the state to undergo training, the state in turn is obliged to the young people to provide some form of training. The fact that activating measures such as the training obligation could also represent a counterproductive additional burden through additional requirements is not discussed. In any case, such compulsory measures in pedagogical contexts lead to situations that are burdened by the compulsory coming together and leave little room for the young people to act according to their own interests and needs (see below).

In Austria, the social investment approach has been of importance (Leibetseder 2016) not only in youth employment promotion (Atzmüller/Knecht 2016a, 2017a). The expansion of pre-school care, the introduction of the compulsory kindergarten year, the discussion about a second compulsory kindergarten year and the increasing documentation of the progress of kindergarten children all point to the growing importance of the social investment approach in early childhood/elementary education (Atzmüller/Décieux/Knecht 2019; Atzmüller/Knecht 2016b). Despite the dominance of the social investment approach, other priorities emerged for the two Black-Blue Coalitions in the employment promotion of young people.

In *both Black-Blue government periods* of the coalitions of the conservative ÖVP and the right-wing populist/extreme right FPÖ, the focus was on measures relating to the resource money and the associated incentive mechanisms as well as to the resource time. The most important measure of the Black-Blue Coalitions to improve the training situation was undoubtedly the launch of the generous subsidies for companies that offered apprenticeship places ("apprenticeship promotion/subsidies"; see also Tab. 3, col. 2 and 3). These were initially distributed according to the "watering can principle"[56] and thus benefited all companies that provided training. In the meantime, additional bonuses for the companies existed, for example, in the exemption from health insurance contributions for apprentices. Thus, positive financial incentives (more financial resources) were mainly used for companies. There were no negative incentives such as the introduction of a standard that companies had to train apprentices and were penalised for non-compliance.

In the case of measures aimed at youths and young adults, both governments placed less emphasis on their support and more on negative financial incentives: for example, the training allowance (and social assistance) was reduced, thus creating greater financial pressure, the number of SCT places was limited and the pay of apprentices working there was reduced. The measures therefore largely follow the idea of negative financial incentives. (An increase of apprentices' salaries, which could also lead to a better coverage of appren-

---

56 https://www.dw.com/en/word-of-the-week-giesskannenprinzip/a-18481157.

ticeships, was not discussed. Such ideas are countered in the context of a deficit-oriented discourse on the "quality" of young people that in that case apprenticeships would hardly be offered anymore). At the same time, both Black-Blue Coalitions set the course for more lavish subsidies for companies that provide training. The negative financial incentives to which apprentices were subjected represent a different form of activation than the training obligation: it is not a punishable requirement but a form of implicit coercion. However, it must be considered that it is precisely the combination of obligation and financial pressure that can turn out to be problematic: Particularly when the obligation to accept an apprenticeship is combined with the threat of a lack of financial means and possibly an insufficient supply of SCT places, apprenticeship seekers are forced into unattractive apprenticeships with high pressure. This then also thwarts the hope expressed in interviews that compulsory training would lead to binding offers.

Beyond the activation through financial pressure and the special way of apprenticeship subventions, the handling of the resource time showed itself as a special feature of the Black-Blue Coalitions: Some of the measures adopted that affect young people relate to the disposal of the resource time. Under Black-Blue I and II, the working hours were extended and made more flexible. The regulation that young people in the SCT have to apply permanently is on the one hand connected with a time expenditure, but also changes the subjective meaning of the measure and possibly stigmatises it. The effects of flexible time policies are not easy to grasp in terms of their significance (and distributional effects), but negative influences on quality of life and well-being are likely (cf. Mairhuber/Atzmüller 2009).

In a way, flexibilisation and its effects for young people correspond to the ideology of the neoliberals that the market should be the framework of society. Nevertheless, these measures are not to be seen only as part of a neoliberal policy of dismantling the welfare state: The promotion or subsidisation of companies that train apprentices was introduced without examining whether the apprenticeships actually were unprofitable; they represent a policy that corresponds to the conservative welfare regime in its strong middle/upper class orientation ("Mittelschicht"/"Mittelstand").

If we look at the discourse analysis and the institutional analysis in an overview, we see that in the discourse analysis the focus is on the lack of psychological/mental resources and the lack of educational resources, which, first of all, those affected have to develop. This discussion of the lack of resources does not correspond to the resource orientation, which particularly wants to emphasise existing resources and their development possibilities. If the discussion of lack of motivation is conducted on a personal level and structural aspects are disregarded, it may also take on a discriminatory character. A lack of material resources and work courage is only attributed secondary importance even by professionals, although empirical studies have proven their limiting effects. At the institutional level, the social investment approach favoured by the SPÖ-ÖVP coalition has gained in importance over the last 20 years. However, education is reduced to formal educational qualifications and hopes are pinned on the idea that more education will automatically lead to less unemployment. On the one hand, the ÖVP-FPÖ coalitions relied heavily on making the labour force more flexible, which had an impact on the daily lives of young apprentices. At the same time, corporate subsidies were introduced. These measures, in their ambivalence, were hardly discussed in public.

5.2 Social inequalities and new divisions – issues of social justice

Beyond the clear differences in the policies of the various government coalitions, it becomes apparent on the one hand that the development of the measures is characterised by a permanent wrangling over detailed regulations, which are hardly dealt with or understood in the public discourse. The respective government and other interest groups (e.g. the social partners) try to launch their view of justice in discourses and implement it institutionally. On the other hand, it can be seen that the development of the measures goes hand in hand with fundamental decisions such as the introduction of the training guarantee and compulsory training, which represent a change in the system and are difficult to reverse, but can at most be modified.

Changes to the detailed regulations sometimes resulted in pendulum movements, in that new regulations were successfully passed in the form of new laws, decrees and ordinances and then reversed or at least modified by the following coalition.[57] Even if these regulations may seem unimportant at first glance, they nevertheless have a considerable impact on the financial situation of the young people concerned, but also, for example, on the subsidised training companies, so that one can use the term "justice of the detailed regulations" for this circumstance, which is indeed the case in practice, but not in theory where it is hardly discussed. If discussed changes are above the public perception threshold, they must be legitimised. Thus, the Ministry of Social Affairs proclaims sweepingly that it has achieved justice with compulsory training/education: The manifold benefits of the so-called *Training up to 18*

> "range from an increase in justice to a considerable increase in GDP (110 million € in 10 years). *Training up to 18* is characterised by the fact that instead of 'more

---

57 This can be seen, for example, in the expansion and reduction of apprenticeship subsidies, in the regulations on employment opportunities for asylum-seeking young people, in the payment of or exemption from health insurance contributions

of the same', alternatives for raising the level of education are also included. Another success of *Training up to 18* lies in a decrease in the NEET rate of 15 to19-year-olds." (SMS 2019)

Social investment logic is usually based on the idea that justice can be established by offering all members equal opportunities – first in the training market and then in the labour market – and that differences in "performance" would then only be due to differences in individual performance (Atzmüller/Knecht 2017a; s. a. Giddens 2000; Lessenich 2004). At the same time, meritocratic logics became more and more prevalent in practice, as the social investment approach and neoliberal policies focused on increasing competitiveness and economic growth (Solga 2012, 2008; Müller 2015). Measures such as training guarantees and compulsory training could in principle lead to more people being well educated, the low-wage sector being thinned out and incomes levelling out. In fact, however, this has only happened to a very small extent in Austria over the last 20 years (Geisberger 2021; Geisberger/Knittler 2010).[58] Changes such as the increase in precarious work (Bohrn Mena 2020), especially the increase in part-time work and the legalisation of temporary and contract work, counteract the idea of creating more income equality through more education. This shows that the attempt to create justice through more educational opportunities or more educational equality – in the form of an isolated solution – has not worked so far (s. a. Cantillon 2011). For the situation in Germany, Solga emphasised in the context of empirical studies that "the role of education as well as the reduction of educational inequalities must not be overestimated as a means of fighting poverty and reducing inequality" and that "direct measures of social redistribution are far more effective than indirect measures affecting the education system" (Solga 2012: 480; s. a. Atzmüller/Knecht 2017a: 125; Butterwegge 2021). State support aimed at higher educational attainment would therefore have to go hand in hand with poverty reduction in order to combat poverty effectively and in the long term.

Contrary to these findings, the public discourses described above indicate that the socio-political distribution discourses and mechanisms have once again intensified, especially at the end of the 20-year period under research, which also has effects on people at the lower end of the income distribution. Within the framework of a policy that discursively turned against benefits for asylum seekers and whose cuts then also reached many other disadvantaged population groups, a reduction of social benefits and rights was pushed forward, which affected the youth sector just as much as the areas of minimum security/social assistance, working time regulations (with the introduction of

---

for apprentices or in the (supra-)company co-determination opportunities for young people within the framework of the Youth Council of Confidence.
58   The size of the low-wage sector, which incidentally can be reduced more directly by a statutory minimum wage, has hardly decreased between 2009 and 2020.

the daily maximum working time of twelve hours) or the second labour market (through the abolition of the *20,000 action for* older unemployed people). On the other hand, new benefits were created, especially for companies, entrepreneurs and high-income earners (Knecht/Bodenstein 2019; Atzmüller/Knecht/Bodenstein 2020). This is a policy that first discursively propagated and promoted a division between the allegedly existing and clearly separable groups of high achievers on the one hand and the allegedly lazy, undisciplined benefit recipients on the other hand (see above and Atzmüller/Knecht 2017a and Wodak 2020). Institutionally, the benefits of social assistance, but also of the SCT, were reduced, which led to a worsening of the situation of those affected and thus to a spreading of the income structure.

In the same period, the introduction of the *Family Bonus Plus* counteracted the reform of social assistance, which, among other things, provided for the capping of expenses for families with many(!) children (Tálos/Obinger 2019: 253). The Austrian *Family Bonus Plus* represents a high tax-free amount for children, the amount of which – unlike the new social assistance – increases proportionally with each child and which produces high tax losses ("opportunity costs"). It targets high-income families and hardly reaches low-income families (Fink/Rocha-Akis 2018, Budget Service of the Parliament of the Republic of Austria 2018; see also Der Standard 2018c and Atzmüller/Knecht/Bodenstein 2020). In fact, the tax losses due to this allowance are larger than all social assistance transfers (for children and adults) combined (Baumgartner et al. 2018), which shows that the combination of measures does not reduce the reach of welfare state regulations, but reaches other, less needy population groups.

The combination of these measures points to a policy of division that assigns different obligations and rights to different population and status groups, which is described in the social policy literature as dualization (Emmenegger et al. 2012; Dallinger/Fückel 2014; Atzmüller/Knecht 2017a: 125). It can be part of a populism that pretends to make a policy "for the people", but in fact, it is as an elitist project, a redistribution in favour of the wealthy and entrepreneurs (cf. also Biskamp 2019) and in doing so weakens rather than strengthens the position of average workers and employees (see e.g. Schenk 2015).

5.3 Right-wing populist/extreme right social policy as a hierarchising and exclusionary policy of prevention

The FPÖ presents itself as a "social homeland party" (Lehner/Wodak 2020: 192) and likes to emphasise its supposedly existing social vein claining that it would take care of "the little man in the street" (actually also less of "the little woman"[59]) (see e.g. Ennser-Jedenastik 2018b). At the same time, however, it is repeatedly shown that political decisions, e.g. in parliament, tend to be taken in favour of privileged population groups (see above as well as Zandonella 2020; Bonvalot 2017; Schenk 2015; Schmid n.d.). Afonso (2015) assumes that this results from the fact that right-wing populist parties often have to form coalitions with conservative parties in order to come to power (s. a. Ennser-Jedenastik 2018b). However, there are clear signs that these ruptures between discourse and politics are due to "double-tongued" politics (cf. also Fischer 2020; Rosenberger/Schmid 2003: 105f.[60]), which tries to organise majorities with simplistic, racist statements, but in doing so pursues goals that may not be oriented towards the interests of their (target group of) voters[61] and perhaps cannot or should not even be named publicly, as they are so-called "forbidden goals" (s. a. Münch 2016: 50, 62; Yanow 1992)[62]

For the case of Austria, Bonvalot points out (2017) that Jörg Haider already called for a dismantling of the welfare state in the 1990s (Haider 1994). However, despite his neoliberal penchant, he focused on specific explanatory patterns such as the prevention of immigration, a promised privileging of the Austrian population, a pro-natalist perspective and, in particular, the exclusion of various population groups, starting with foreigners, asylum seekers, but also

---

59   The far-right policies of the FPÖ deal only rudimentarily with women's policy and only very selectively with issues in the context of family (see e.g. Löffler 2018; Schmid n.d.). Often these policies are anti-feminist and envisage a traditional (family) role for women; at the same time, there is a focus on men's policies (see Mayrhofer 2006).

60   Rosenberger and Schmid write about the policies of the first ÖVP-FPÖ government: "The measures and the discourses about these measures fall apart" (Rosenberger/Schmid 2003: 105) and "The orientation of poverty and exclusion policies expresses the divergence of measures and public discourse very clearly." (Rosenberger/Schmid 2003: 110).

61   In Austria, this discussion is linked to the question of whether the Ibiza scandal is only the visible iceberg of a policy that is the essence of the FPÖ, whether exactly the opposite is the case, or in what ways the two tendencies might be intertwined. There was comparatively little discussion of the fact that it might seem inconsistent that a decidedly racist and anti-elitist vice chancellor who criticises the press and presents himself as a "clean man" negotiates with a Russian (!) oligarch (!) about the takeover of a tabloid (!) and obviously illegal donation and barter deals. There were voices that there might be certain voters who could identify with this action, which transgressed borders and laws. The revelations about the financing of his living costs by expenses paid by the party, which became public only a short time later, seemed to be considered immoral by the population to a higher degree. (In the spirit of Austrian law, it is added here that the presumption of innocence applies.)

62   Among other things, the Austrian variant of right-wing populist/extreme right politics raises the question of whether the FPÖ had not pragmatically accommodated companies that it had in mind as possible sources of funding for its own party (see for such events in Hungary and Poland: Becker 2023) or hoped to gain advantages in the context of privatisations. (Schmidt 2018) or through appointments to positions in large companies.

so-called "welfare parasites" (Bonvalot 2017; s. a. Obinger/Tálos 2006; Tálos 2004; Rosenberger/Schmid 2003). With the first Black-Blue coalition government, labour (protection) rights were restricted and the possibilities for their enforcement, especially by trade unions, were limited (Bonvalot 2017: 35).

With regard to the employment promotion of disadvantaged young people, it has already been shown above (chapter 5.2 and 5.3) that the policies of the Black-Blue governments particularly focused on and served the interests of businesses, but that this was little discussed in public. In contrast, the education, training and employment policy for asylum-seeking young people was brought into the focus of the public interest, although this only affected about 1,000 of about 100,000 apprentices (see tab. 2). As already mentioned, asylum-seeking young people have hardly any access to education and further training opportunities after completing compulsory schooling: They were excluded from the training guarantee and the training obligation. access to integration measures such as language courses and trainings, which was expanded under the Red-Black Government, was made more difficult again in 2018 (Atzmüller/Knecht/Bodenstein 2020). By abolishing the possibility to complete an apprenticeship in shortage of occupations (see above, chapter 4.3), the exclusion policy towards young asylum seekers was strengthened in 2018. This step followed the announcement in the government's programme:

> "All opportunities should be open to our youth. Our children should be able to grow up to become mature, responsible citizens. The aim is to promote their development as independent personalities in order to lead an independent life and to be able to optimally use and develop their potentials and talents. It is extremely important that young people have a positive perspective for the future. Policymakers must do everything in their power to ensure that this is the case." (ÖVP/FPÖ 2017: 101)

"Our youth" and "Our children" can be read here as an announcement of a discriminatory, exclusionary child and youth policy: In this case, the gap between Austrian children and young people, whose privileges have been extended, and asylum-seeking children and young people, who are increasingly denied the aforementioned opportunities, has been widened. (cf. Knecht/Bodenstein 2019). Deliberate marginalisation goes beyond "mere" nativist welfare chauvinism, i.e. a marginalisation of population groups of other nations in the distribution of welfare benefits (Atzmüller/Knecht/Bodenstein 2020; Atzmüller 2022; Jørgensen/Thomsen 2016; Koning 2019; Keskinen 2016; Stubbs/Lendvai-Bainton 2020), not only at the discursive level. Exclusionary strategies have also been deliberately used beyond the distribution of (monetary) benefits. If the lack of integration leads to problems, this is, in case of doubt, grist to the mill of right-wing populists (Sator 2018).

The ban on doing an apprenticeship in a shortage occupation, as well as the plans to simultaneously extend the access of young third-country nationals to apprenticeships in shortage occupations by extending the scope of the Red-White-Red Card to apprentices (see ÖVP/FPÖ 2017; Szigetvari 2018a; Der Standard 2018c) can be read as a further aspect of a small-scale allocation of rights (and obligations) that creates new differences – here between asylum seekers and non-EU nationals – and new social inequalities: an "exchange" of asylum-seeking apprentices for shortage occupation apprenticeships by third-country nationals with a Red-White-Red Card would have meant improved access for the latter, but residence in Austria with a Red-White-Red Card categorically precludes access to social benefits such as the minimum income scheme (cf. Knecht/Bodenstein 2019). Such processes also produce further hierarchies of rights and obligations between different groups of people.

In addition to the restriction of the possibilities to use education and training offers, other rights of basic social security were also reduced or differentiated: Since 2016, young people and adults entitled to subsidiary protection have only been granted core social assistance benefits that do not exceed the level of basic provision (Woltran 2018).[63] People who received a humanitarian right to stay were granted the status of Red-White-Red Card holders, which entails extensive exclusion from social benefits. In addition to the explicit exclusion of asylum-seeking young people from the education and training system, a system of multi-level, temporary or provisional allocation of rights has been created that keeps people in limbo and insecure. The graduated attribution of rights can be described as hierarchisation (see for Germany: Pichl 2017; s. a. Horvath 2014). This hierarchisation corresponds with the social order and hierarchical ideas of far-right parties.

From the perspective of Resource Theory, exclusion from the education system as well as the (accompanying) denial of recognition and of psychological and social resources (through exclusion from school, work, etc.) is an important part of these policies. It is not only about cutting benefits, but also about preventing people from using and building up resources. Considerations within the framework of Resource Theory thus refer to a specific connection between policies on the allocation of resources and policies on the use of resources. This is particularly evident in the example of the reduced funding for language courses for asylum seekers. With regard to the institutional implementation of border exclusion policy, however, it also becomes apparent that it is not only a matter of the category 'foreigner', but also of measures which are characterised by an understanding of human beings that combines racist-exclusionary motives with a benefit-oriented view of human beings (Kourabas/Mecheril 2022: 15; Horvath 2014): For example, as already mentioned, it was not only discussed to abolish the possibility for asylum-seeking young people to com-

---

63 An attempt to reduce benefits for these temporary beneficiaries of asylum was contradicted by the ECJ (Woltran 2018, Sußner 2018, European Court of Justice 2018).

plete an apprenticeship in a shortage occupation, but also to consider extending the Red-White-Red Card to young people from third countries. The presence of people from third countries is apparently considered unproblematic as long as they are largely disenfranchised, because holders of the Red-White-Red Card have to leave the country again at the end of their employment and thus have hardly any access to social benefits. Thus, a system of gradual exclusion is installed that functions in the sense of calculating economic benefits or exploiting people. In the context of this calculation, the parallel marginalisation and exclusion of certain groups of nationals who appear to be less useful also becomes understandable.

5.4 Thinking the welfare state "from below"

Social policy is often understood as an authority that intervenes on the basis of rights to benefit the (basic) needs of citizens. Thus Marshall (1992) conceived of the development of the status of citizens in the (welfare) state as a progressive expansion of civic, political and social rights. And Kaufmann described social policy as "state induced measures" with "determinable effects with reference to the 'social conditions'" (Kaufmann 2005: 86). He distinguished four forms of intervention: firstly, measures to improve the legal status of persons; secondly, measures to improve the income situation, so-called economic interventions; thirdly, measures to improve the social infrastructure, such as the construction of parks or social services; fourthly, pedagogical measures that improve the ability and willingness of persons to act (Kaufmann 2005: ch. 3.2).

The fact that education and training measures play an increasingly important role in social policy, especially in the context of the social investment approach, leads to shifts: The "accumulation of human capital" requires the participation of the citizens or clients concerned can only come into being in an act of co-production (e.g. Schwarze 2012: 122f.). If politicians are suspicious of the cooperation of citizens, they try to introduce mechanisms of activation, control or coercion[64] – and this is exactly what happened with the transition of the training guarantee to the training obligation in 2017. But such measures could also be thought of in a participatory way and be more efficiently oriented towards the needs and interests of those affected.

The perspective "from below" (Steinert/Pilgram 2003; Bareis/Wagner 2015; Bareis 2020) criticises the reification of those affected by the adminis-

---

64 Various modes can be distinguished here: firstly, the linking of benefits to additional preconditions and "tests of fitness" (Dörre et al. 2013), secondly, positive incentive mechanisms (payments/benefits/bonuses), thirdly, negative incentive mechanisms (deductions), fourthly, prohibitions without and with the threat of punishment, fifthly, regulations enforced with coercion.

tration (and also by research) and asks how competently those affected deal with this reification (Bareis/Cremer-Schäfer 2013: 149), to which extend they make use of services and offers for themselves and which hurdles and impositions have to be overcome in everyday life (ibid.). This perspective focuses on the interactions between those affected and state or social institutions and examines the strategies and the stubbornness of those affected as agents. Resources that help them cope with everyday life play a special role in this approach. In this respect, this perspective can be linked to resource-theoretical approaches, which argue that resources only acquire their value with regard to their use and the goals pursued. If a person finds the use of resources and a commitment attractive against the background of his or her own goals, then he or she will also decide to do so voluntarily.

It is again the discourses about the misuse of social benefits and about the alleged low motivation of young people that oppose the idea of offering measures in a participatory framework and on a voluntary basis, as an interview of the SocIEtY project with a senior official reveals:

"For example, how do you set up a concrete project design [...] without the whole thing getting out of hand, to strengthen the participation of the apprentices. Because basically there are obligations [i.e. participation in a qualification measure – note: A.K.] because it costs money – and there is this contradiction [with] voluntariness. [...] If they get a recommendation for a measure, which is agreed upon anyway, and they refuse, then they usually get a tenner from the AMS [= Austrian Public Employment Service], a punishment – withdrawal of benefits! [...] He gets a suspension of benefits. [...] He gets his social aid payment blocked [...], if he refuses, for example, to accept an offer of employment [...]." (Interview of the SocIEtY project, as cited in Knecht/Atzmüller 2017: 251).

It seems, therefore, that greater trust in "the youth" on the part of the administration, politicians, professionals and the population as a whole would be necessary to make more participatory projects conceivable and possible.

Regardless of whether in practice rather authoritarian, activating measures or participatory, emancipation-promoting measures are implemented, the change of the welfare state leads to the fact that a theory of welfare state interventions delve more deeply into the behaviour, actions and agency of the population, and that a theory of citizen-state interactions should be further developed within the framework of a perspective or of the "welfare state 'from below'" or user orientation.

6 Impact of socio-political change on social work and on young people

This chapter addresses the impact of socio-political change on social work in the field of employment support for disadvantaged young people and on the young people themselves. While chapter 6.1 discusses changes in the context of social investment labour market policies, chapter 6.2 addresses the impact of right-wing populist policies. Chapter 6.3 goes into depth on the analysis of the effects on young people and chapter 6.4 focuses on the (lack of) opportunities for participation in the area of employment support for young people.

6.1 Changing social pedagogy of transition through social investment labour market policy

The introduction of the training guarantee in 2007 brought about a steady expansion of employment support for disadvantaged young people. This led to a large number of career-promoting offers and, statistically speaking, to a "good 'supply situation' for young people" (Knecht 2014: 228) and has been a factor for the comparatively low number of unemployed young people, early school leavers and NEETs. The expansion of Supra-Company Training (SCT) as well as the expansion of production schools or the *Ausbildungsfit* programme and Youth Coaching led to a relative increase in the importance of employment measures in the context of youth policy interventions. Compared to open youth work – i.e. youth work in youth centres and youth clubs and outreach youth work in public spaces – and compared to school social work, the area of employment promotion grew disproportionately (ibid.; cf. also Tab. 3, col. 1). Although services such as Youth Coaching claim to offer comprehensive personal help, they always deal with personal problems in the context of labour market support and its objectives (see also Sanduvac, 2014; cf. also Tab. 3, col. 1) (s. a. Sanduvac 2018). In view of the social work and socio-educational orientation of the measures presented, it became apparent that the boundaries between youth work and employment promotion were increasingly blurred by newly developed concepts and that the two areas were becoming more closely interlinked (Knecht 2014). The pressure on open youth work – which was increasingly confronted with youth unemployment and the uncertainty of the transition from school to employment (Krisch 2011: 507) – to cover labour market-related topics such as writing letters of application increased.[65] Social

---

65 For Austria: Knecht 2014; Knecht/Atzmüller 2017: S. 243; for Europe: European Commission 2015.

pedagogical (leisure) offers were quasi activated in order to lead the young people to the training and labour market. For open youth work, which sees itself as biased in favour of the side of young people and works on the development and empowerment of young people, this new role presents irritation (ebd; Oehme/Beran/Krisch 2007).[66] Here one could speak of a colonisation of youth work. However, there were also positive reports of an improved exchange between open youth work and institutions of labour market promotion, through which the views and understanding of open youth work could be communicated to the labour administration (Knecht 2014: 227).

For the young people, access to the measures represents an educational resource that is, in a sense, linked to a "quid pro quo", a counter transaction. Young people are promised integration into society through success in the labour markets – provided they adopt certain behaviours and orientations (including fulfilling training duty) that are understood as rational, mature and adult (Atzmüller/Knecht 2017a). In this context, compulsory training/education includes activating and punitive components. The contexts of coercion have intensified (s. a. Kähler/Zobrist 2013; Gehrmann/Müller 2010) with the new training duty having little impact on pupils in secondary schools, but affecting disadvantaged young people in particular ("dualization") (see also Sting/Knecht 2022). The invocations (Althusser 1977) and measures do not follow the principle of the *entrepreneurial self* (Bröckling 2007), which presupposes self-optimisation and self-disciplining and to which graduates of higher schools are more likely to be exposed (ibid; Knecht/Atzmüller 2017: 247). For disadvantaged youth the interventions rather correspond to an activating logic of demanding and promoting and thus represent a form of activation policy.

Using the example of Youth Coaching, which is officially considered a voluntary offer (SMS 2021) but within the framework of compulsory training for young people who cannot be in training for various reasons, it can be shown how voluntary guidance services can also become part of an activation and punishment system. The guideline that counselling should be voluntary, open-ended and silent (Schubert/Rohr/Zwicker-Pelzer 2019: 15, 209f.) is no longer

---

66 However, it is also the professionals who are in contact with the young people who express dissenting voices and question, for example, the sense of increasing commitment and activation – but also of transition management in general: "That is also a bit of my criticism [...] of this transition management. That people no longer ask what young people actually want: 'Do they want that? Do they want this kind of training?' Isn't it also a sign that [...] the number of those who drop out of the apprenticeship in the first year is totally high. ... It's neither fun nor do you get recognition. [...] And therefore one could [...] heretically say that this transition management tries very hard to get young people to strive for apprenticeships and to say: 'Yes, I'm striving for this apprenticeship myself'. But whether that is what appeals to young people, one can doubt." (Interview of the SocIEtY Project, quoted in Knecht 2016: 854)

fulfilled. However, the punitive mechanisms do not take place for the most part in the concrete cooperation between professionals and young people, but are outsourced. For example, the compulsory training is administered by separate regional "Training up to 18 Coordination Centres". When these offices have identified young people who are not in training or care, they commission the organisations that carry out Youth Coaching to make contact and provide care. However, the penalties imposed in the case of suspected lack of the will to cooperate are mediated via the coordination offices and the administration. This at least relieves the relationship of the youth coaches to their clients and gives them the chance to try to establish the paradox of an apparent freedom of action within a coercive context. Nevertheless, these counselling sessions always take place under the Damocles sword of punishment. Therefore, the increasingly activating, punitive and controlling character of welfare state interventions (as well as the discriminatory discourses that form the basis of their introduction) can hinder trusting, appreciative cooperation. Maier (2013) uses a German study to show the great importance of at least partial voluntariness for young people who have often had difficult experiences with the coercive school system (see also Knecht 2014: 224f.).

In the final analysis, it is irrelevant for the situation of young people which problem descriptions played a central role in the arguments for the introduction of compulsory training/education – mental problems, lack of skilled workers or long-term securing of the offer of help. For them, the resource-allocating offers are linked to various obligations and a threat of punishment. Instead of viewing adolescence in terms of the 'adolescent moratorium' as a phase of experimentation, self-expression and protest, it is constructed as a transitional phase in which the development of marketable skills and smooth integration into the work world are paramount, undermining the understanding of this phase of life as one of latency, experimentation and nonconformity (see Sting/ Knecht 2022; Knecht/Atzmüller 2019). The orientation of socio-educational and social work activities towards future employability and human capital formation through a shift towards activation policies and vocational training resulted in state and para-state institutions having a broad grasp on children and young people and their subjectivity (Atzmüller/Décieux/Knecht 2019). In addition to young people, this already affects children in crèches and kindergartens (see ibid.).

In this context, the vocational training measures were designed in such a way that they were officially intended to train job-related skills, especially manual skills, following, however a "secret curriculum" (Hoff/Lappe/Lempert 1982: 530) whith the aim is of enduring certain frustrations without giving up the apprenticeship (see e.g. quotation from the SocIEtY project in Knecht/Atzmüller 2017: 247). Ultimately, it is (also) about learning to cope with the demands of flexibilised and precarious labour markets in a subordinate position.

From the point of view of resource orientation and theory, it becomes clear that in the context of the transformation from a providing to a socially investing and activating welfare state, the notion of the resource-allocating state must be supplemented by an analysis of the preconditions attached to the utilisation of benefits and services, i.e. conditionalisation. Welfare state services become a "business" of very unequal partners, because in the relationship between state and citizen, it is the state that sets the conditions. "Agreements" and "contracts" that are becoming more and more common, especially in the field of labour market integration, deceive conceptually about the power imbalance of these relationships, as they do not correspond at all to a usual client relationship.

6.2 The quasi-pedagogy of the market and right-wing populist/extreme-right exclusionary politics

While the Red-Black Coalition focused on supporting young people and channelling their life courses, the policy of the Black-Blue Coalition can be seen as an attempt to expose young people more to the market, which is then supposed to take on a quasi-educational function – in the form of increased constraints. The company becomes the primary place of learning (s. a. Dehnbostel 2020; Gonon 2002).

Already during the first coalition, policies of apprenticeship subsidies, benefits and flexibilization of wage labour were established on a larger scale (see above, chapter 4.1). After 2017, the policy of subsidising apprenticeships went hand in hand with a reduction in pay in supra-company training, furthermore with the compulsion to permanently apply for company apprenticeships, with sanctioning by cancelling the "covering of subsistence" or unemployment benefit, and with a reduction in funding for labour market policy measures. Among others, this policy of pushing back and referring to the insufficient apprenticeships possibly pushes young people into unsuitable or unattractive apprenticeships through increased pressure. Higher pressure then replaces pedagogical interventions, so to speak. The "market" and the company, in combination with the pressure of threatened sanctions, become quasi-pedagogical institutions themselves. This closely follows the ideas of the neoliberal (pre-)thinkers who see the market economy as the framework of a society in which the state does not disappear but remains present – in a different way: "The state does not develop into a 'weak minimal state' at all, but remains a 'strong state'." (Hammerschmidt 2014: 329f; Götsch/Kessl 2017: 183; cf. Foucault 2004). The market is supposed to induce certain required behaviours in the population. The approach of the Black-Blue Coalition thus also corresponds to the views of analysts and critics of neoliberalism, who describe its essence within the framework of neo-social governmentality as a change in the form of rule

(Kessl/Otto 2002; 2003; Lessenich 2009: 166, 2008: 14, 84f; Lutz 2010; Ziegler 2009).

The policy has a different effect on young people seeking asylum. Here, the policy does not attempt to create integration via the market. Admittedly, the young people are also subject to requirements, such as the obligations of the Integration Act and the Integration Year Act (e.g. learning the language, "cultural adaptation"), the reduction of social welfare in the case of poor German language skills, the incentives through voluntary, low-paid work to improve their prospects in the asylum procedure. If their application is rejected, they may be subject to compulsory residence, the threat of coercive detention or deportation (Austrian National Assembly 2017b). However, these measures obviously do not serve the purpose of integration, but primarily of harassment and deterrence – also of other potential asylum seekers (see e.g. Borrelli/Bochsler 2020; Lindberg 2020). The fact that this type of policy is not at all interested in integration also became visible through the reduction of funds for the measures of the 2018 Integration Act.

Accordingly, social work with young asylum seekers represents an extreme form of 'exclusivity-administering social work'.[67] Social workers in this field work in an environment where the integration and inclusion of their clients is hindered rather than promoted. The daily rates for the accommodation of unaccompanied asylum-seeking minors (UMF) in Austria are unlawfully lower than for Austrian children (Austrian National Assembly 2020b). Even before 2015, Stemberger and colleagues asked how social work in this context could at all "sustainably expand opportunities for participation in society and their personal development" (Stemberger/Katsivelaris/Zirkowitsch 2014: 37) can. Under the given conditions, "the practical implementation of this goal appears to be an ideal state towards which one is oriented, but which cannot be achieved. The small resources made available by primary care are not sufficient to fulfil a mission guided by professional ethics" (ibid.). In addition to the problem of restricted access to the labour market, further reports (Wagner 2020; Schmidhofer 2013) and scandals (Der Standard 2022) point to persistent non-child-friendly and non-youth-friendly conditions in the context of the asylum procedure as well as in camps, which also contradict children's rights (Kindeswohl-Kommission 2021; Drljic/Holzer 2017; Freller 2022).

Thus, while in a labour market policy setting the young people tend to be cared for and counselled due to the influences of an activating social investment policy, the policy of the Black-Blue ÖVP-FPÖ coalition strengthened the market and the company as a quasi-pedagogical framework. In contrast, the policy for asylum-seeking youths, which is primarily intended to serve as a deterrent, leads to a financially under-resourced deficiency administration. For the asylum-seeking youths, who are kept away from the labour market, this

---

67 On the term: Bommes and Scherr 1996; on the situation in Austria: Stemberger et al. 2014.

kind of "custodial social pedagogy and social work" leads to a general lack of perspective, in which professional orientation and vocational learning are hardly possible and everyday life consists of waiting (Bodenstein/Knecht 2017; Knecht/Bodenstein 2019).

For the professionals, pedagogical work is hardly possible any more within the framework of a financially under-resourced shortage administration (Stemberger/Katsivelaris/Zirkowitsch 2014). As a result, resource orientation as an attitude and method can hardly be lived any more, which is equally dependent on a professional approach in contact with young people and children as well as on an appropriate organisational environment that itself requires sufficient resources.

6.3 Discrimination and lack of recognition as problems of young people and as an issue of social work

In the third chapter it was shown that the pathologizing deficit orientation of the professionals partly overlaps with the images of unmotivated young people and deficit parents in the public discourse. While these images of young people are very present, there is little public – and professional – discussion of the fact that different groups of disadvantaged young people are exposed to experiences of discrimination, which can have a major impact on the young people themselves as well as on their motivation and perception of self-efficacy.

Young people experience such discrimination at school (Bauer/Kainz 2007; IDB 2016–2019; Wellgraf 2018), in counselling settings (AG Jugendforschung 2018), on the training market (Knecht 2014: 231; AG Jugendforschung 2018) and in public (ZARA 2000–2010). Especially students with a migration background report individual experiences of discrimination such as insults. However, complaints usually remain without consequences (ORF 2021). Only recently has there been a regularly published discrimination report for the school sector (IDB 2016–2019). Young people are also discriminated against on the training market: youth coaches report of companies that would not hire foreign apprenticeship applicants "on principle" (AG Jugendforschung 2018; s. a. Biffl/Skrivanek 2014; Kapeller/Stiftinger 2014). Nevertheless, the problems of young people in the search for apprenticeships are more likely to be located in the individual failure of the young people (see also. Stajić/Gächter 2012.

For young people, the situation is aggravated by the fact that even sympathetic professionals sometimes tend not to take the experiences reported by young people seriously (enough) in terms of their consequences for the people concerned (Kourabas/Mecheril 2022: 17). The fact that some professionals reflect little on their own behaviour with regard to discrimination and stigmatisation is also reflected in statements made by youth coaches: In the interviews, they stated that they did not consider the use of Youth Coaching to be stigmatising, but when asked, they explained that they would not pull the young people out of class or would rather make appointments in the afternoon in order to protect them from reactions from fellow pupils (AG Jugendforschung 2018).

A special form of institutional discrimination is the promotion of girls in apprenticeships with a low proportion of women. Companies receive 400 € per month if they employ girls in apprenticeships with a low proportion of women. This is an *affirmative action* or "positive discrimination" to compensate for disadvantage. One argument for this design could be the (discriminatory?) assumption that girls would be less effective in these occupations. However, the measure could also have been introduced with the intention of proactively counteracting discriminatory perceptions of apprenticeship providers. (Their prejudices would thus be rewarded.) It is also conceivable that apprenticeship providers persuade interested girls to accept such a position in the hope of gaining funding. The Austrian Federal Economic Chamber actually sees the goal of this support as being "to enable certain disadvantaged groups to enter into an apprenticeship relationship" (WKO 2022b). "This is intended to counteract the gender-specific division of the apprenticeship market." (WKO 2022a) Ultimately, this type of support could also have the effect that the apprenticeship providers are confirmed in their prejudices by the existence of this support. It is questionable whether the desired steering effect would not be greater if female apprentices received 400 € per month if they chose an apprenticeship in an occupation that is classified as typically male, or if support measures were financed to reduce prejudices.

Young people who are discriminated against, e.g. on the basis of their educational or migrant background, are permanently challenged to behave in the face of these appeals regarding their allegedly lower abilities (Wellgraf 2014). Jürgen Link introduced the term "*dispositional subjectivity*" to describe such specific subjectivities (Link 2007: 224). This refers to the emergence of a person's identity, which is determined from the outside (Knecht 2010: 185; Bührmann/Schneider 2008: 68f.). Studies on mainstream pupils and pupils with a migration background show the functioning of subtle exclusion mechanisms such as denied recognition, withheld support and encouragement, and withheld social affiliations and shaming (Herwartz-Emden et al. 2008: 34; Juhasz/Mey 2003; Wellgraf 2014). Young people's view of themselves depends on how they are seen by society or what assumptions they have about it (see also Fanon 1982; Hall 1996): Wellgraf shows in his studies of main stream pupils in hotspot schools in Germany how the portrayal of these pupils in the media affects them. As a result, they are confronted with a special task of coping with their identity – namely, being a pupil at a focal point school in the media (Wellgraf 2014; 2018). Against this background, it becomes clear that in Austria, too, the problematic attributions of pedagogical professionals in schools, in the offers of employment promotion as well as in the media can have a lasting influence on young people, even if there are few empirical studies on this in Austria (however: Schönherr et al. 2019).

To be recognised as a person in one's own right is a fundamental human need (Honneth 1992; Pregel 2013: 30; Knecht 2016: 850). Especially for young people, whose self-image is not yet as solid as that of adults, recognition of their person and their wishes (e.g. career aspirations) by teachers and other caregivers is an important dimension for their personal development (cf. Andresen 2010: 508; Preite 2019). From the young people's point of view, the recognition of the person and the consideration of their individual wishes, interests and needs are also a prerequisite for helpful interventions. Thus Gaupp (2013) stated that support can only be perceived as helpful by young people under these conditions (Knecht 2016: 851).

In the context of the resource perspective, recognition is not an individual resource, but an interpersonal or relational aspect of the development of psychological/mental resources (Schubert/Knecht 2012: 15) such as the development of motivation and self-efficacy. Knecht (2016) points out the importance of self-efficacy when entring into education and training and he specifies that motivation is volatile and depends on more or less affirming life circumstances. (Low) motivation should therefore be understood not as a characteristic of a person, but as a resource that results from personal contacts as well as from attributions, e.g. being a member of a disadvantaged population group (Lehmkuhl/Schmidt/ Schöler 2013; Wellgraf 2014). Such resources are developed differently at different times or phases of life and are available to varying degrees.

If some approaches to resource activation seem to assume that necessary resources are available but are not (sufficiently) used and only need to be activated, *Resource Theory* and (methodological) resource-oriented action should be aware that lacking resources such as motivation or self-efficacy can also arise from a social blocking of external resources: through lack of recognition of work qualifications, lack of work permits, lack of access via established networks or exclusion when jobs are awarded. With regard to a further development of the Resource Theory, it is accordingly necessary – also following Finis Siegler (2018) – that the level of interaction, which stands for the communication between social worker/social pedagogue and client and their coproduction, must be considered more strongly (see also Fig. 1). Here – within the framework of *street-level bureaucracy* – interactions take place that can be more paternalistic or more "at eye level", that can be frustrating or strengthening, that can cause more or less resistance and/or that can promote positive developments. In the context of concrete support in practice, help would be needed that includes the empowering perspectives of *anti-discrimination pedagogy* or *social justice training,* e.g. by addressing discrimination, stigmatisation and, where appropriate, issues of solidarity.[68]

6.4 Lack of opportunities for participation and the possibility of vocational political training

The discussion of the framework conditions of social pedagogical and social work activities also includes the question of which opportunities for participation or co-determination are provided for young people, among other things because such opportunities are often created within the framework of social projects. It becomes apparent that the extent of the participation opportunities granted differs in different areas of social pedagogy and social work: In the surveys conducted within the framework of the SocIEtY project (Knecht/Kuchler/Atzmüller 2014) it was stated by the open youth work that young people can have a say in various activities of the youth centres and that they can participate in decisions of districts or municipalities through so-called youth parliaments or youth councils (Knecht 2014: 232; s. a. Hellein/Sturm/Hochreiter 2014). In Vienna, for example, such projects have been organised by the youth centres and in other municipalities they have been accompanied by youth facilitators (e.g. Verein Wiener Jugendzentren 2008; Heimgartner 2009: 70ff.) Young people should be given the chance to agree on common relevant topics, to form an opinion and to learn to represent it (Knecht/Kuchler/Atzmüller 2014). With such projects, the responsible ministries implement the EU Youth Strategy (2010–2018 and 2019–2027) (Bundeskanzleramt 2021) which is intended to promote the participation and involvement of young people. In the public media, young people are often portrayed as politically weary and uninterested, although studies show that this is partly true for interest and participation in official elections, but should not be understood as a general lack of political interest (Zimmermann 2010: 195). In particular, projects in which young people experience that involvement makes sense and is taken seriously motivate them to stay involved (ibid.).

In contrast to the participation opportunities described in the context of (open) youth work, the co-determination and control opportunities for young people in the labour market context prove to be very limited:[69] With the proximity to the field of education and work, the opportunities for co-determination dwindle (see for Austria: Knecht 2014) although the Austrian institution of the *Youth Confidence Councils* (in German: "Jugendvertrauensräte"; see above) promotes co-determination in companies and – in parallel – in Supra-Company

---

68   See also the Austrian thematic website: Am Rand 2022.
69   See the discussion on a German example: Enggruber/Fehlau 2021.

Training (see above). And indeed, it is shown that satisfaction is higher in companies where a youth council of confidence has been established (Lachmayr/Mayerl 2019: 10). Nevertheless, the participation opportunities of young people in the labour market-related sector must be classified as rather low. This is shown, among other things, by the fact that young people have no say whatsoever in which occupations they are trained in within the Supra-Company Training; this is determined by the employers' and employees' representatives as social partners. The *Austrian Federal Youth Representation* (in German: "Österreichische Bundesjugendvertretung") is not involved, although formally it has the status of a social partner (Zimmermann 2010: 194). Also, in the qualification measures that are used by those young people who have difficulties finding an apprenticeship and do not attend secondary school, there are usually not even co-determination structures in the form of class/course representatives or similar. Only the AMS has a complaints office, but young people hardly know about it (Knecht 2014: 232). In an interview, an AMS employee referred to evaluations within the framework of a "client monitoring system", some of which has been carried out by external market research institutes. She also mentioned that in Vienna, focus groups had been considered. However, such groups only mean that typical feedback mechanisms of quality assurance are implemented instead of co-determination options (ibid.). In evaluations of measures by means of focus groups or questionnaires, opinions can be expressed and negative experiences reported, However, in contrast to original co-determination possibilities, there is neither the possibility of influencing or criticising the ongoing programmes nor the possibility of influencing one's own living conditions in such surveys. The information collected serves only the experts in the administration, who may then design future measures differently (ibid.). Surveys are, however, taken as an opportunity to claim that information was obtained in a participatory process (cf. Wagner 2014).

The limited opportunities for participation are largely unreflectively supported by the professionals and experts in the field of labour market support. In our interviews, many of them were critical in principle of co-determination opportunities in measures for young people, especially because they see these measures precursors for a working life in which participation is not important and frustration tolerance is a necessary secondary virtue:

> "So what use is it if I say that he can have a say and if it doesn't go so well, he can leave, stupid – it doesn't happen in the company. So, that is [...] such a field of tension in which we all move and where one probably always moves." (Interview of the SocIEtY project, as cited in Knecht 2014: 224)

> "... That means I have to put up with some trainer or some workshop manager nagging at me every day, but that's just the way life is. I also have to put up with my boss when she nags and clubs me, is it like this? But yeah, can't say stupid ... now I'm going home for two hours." (Interview of the SocIEtY project, as cited in Atzmüller/Knecht 2016a: 126)

The fact that many professional activities and experiences of young people often leave little room for self-realisation partly reinforces – for example in the context of open youth work – the contradiction between a professional claim to work with young people in an empowering, emancipatory and self-efficacy-promoting way and the task of preparing them for the demands of the labour market (Knecht 2014: 229). The established system prevents the experience of self-efficacy, as a leading administrative also suggests in the interview:

> "Well, we are currently surveying participant satisfaction [...], but always afterwards, that's a quality assurance thing. ... That would have to be discussed, this feedback culture – which is also a learning process for the young people, to develop such a feedback culture." (Interview of the SocIEtY project, as cited in Knecht 2016: 856)

In this way, experiences of self-empowerment, co-determination and solidarity as well as opportunities to formulate alternative ideas of justice are systematically prevented and young people are thrown back on individual strategies of adaptation (Knecht/Atzmüller 2019; Otto et al. 2017). This also shows the problem that the experiences and problems in the search for an apprenticeship and a job are individualised within the framework of counselling services such as Youth Coaching and are not discussed as a political issue at any point.

The lack of opportunities for co-determination is surprising insofar as in the relevant literature (e.g. Walther 2006: 217, 2019; Enggruber/Fehlau 2021) co-determination in the creation and implementation of measures is considered a suitable way of increasing motivation; various ways of involvement are also suggested (e.g. in the form of class spokespersons, course spokespersons, ombudspersons or quality circles of all participants, in hearing procedures in the authority state administrative action, in unemployment councils or in self- or cooperatively organised offers (e.g. Schwarze 2012: 158).

Instead of further developing the programmes within the framework of participatory and democratic structures, the training guarantee and training duty programmes are increasingly collecting data the course of casework and evaluationg them. Young people's lives are increasingly penetrated in a quantifying way. At the same time, there is little research on the subjective understanding of the young people concerned; expenditure on vocational education and training research that goes beyond evaluations and is integrated into vocational education and training research also remains low (Hesse et al. 2019; Gruber 2008).

Orientation towards a broader understanding of education, which would offer young people the opportunity to experience their living environment not only as an economic but also as a social and political space that opens up a variety of life plans and individual life possibilities, could offer young people the opportunity to practise democratic co-determination (Knecht/Atzmüller 2019: 228). In contrast, the reduction to a necessary "post-maturation" addressed in training policy activities restricts the space for reflection on one's own living conditions to *employability* and marketability, instead of individual and social emancipation and autonomy (Betzelt 2019; Betzelt/Bothfeld 2014; Knecht/Schenk 2023) as goals.

7 Conclusion and outlook

This study examines how employment support for disadvantaged young people as part of social policy changed in Austria between the years 2000 and 2020 and what impact this change has had on the framework conditions of social pedagogues, social workers and other professionals working in this field as well as on young people. For this purpose, the change of relevant discourses (in chapter 3) as well as the institutional changes (in chapter 4) were examined. Within the theoretical framework of the Resource Theory, the analysis of discourses, models and institutional changes serves to describe the change in employment support for disadvantaged young people. Chapter 5 investigates the significance of the change for the welfare state, and Chapter 6 the effects on social work and those affected.

With regard to the method, it could be shown that the analysis of the relationship between politics and social education/social work can be supplemented and advanced with the chosen approach. The resource-theoretical approach allows for a broad analysis of both social inequality and the chosen measures by looking at the spectrum of resources. The separate but intertwined consideration of discourses and institutions revealed, for example, the emphasis on the lack of psychological/mental resources of young people in the legitimisation of measures as well as the observation that the implemented measures do not directly address these deficits, but are only carried out in relation to the labour market. The analysis of the guiding principles made it possible to make socio-political change understandable in larger contexts. Discursive elements, such as the reduced view of employability of the social investment approach or the emphasis on monetary incentive mechanisms of the neoliberal model, shape the policies that are implemented. The extension of the idea of distribution of resources, has made to things apparent: the importance of measures that aim to prevent the use of existing resources with exclusionary intentions and the fact that social policy can and should also be considered "from the bottom up" – in several ways. *Co-production* and *participation* point to changed approaches and perspectives in social policy, through which those affected are more involved. In the context of social policy change in recent years, however, it is apparent that involvement through activation and the threat of punishment more prominently determine the possibilities of participation. The methods and results complement existing analyses, which are often oriented towards the concept of welfare regimes and compare various countries (Walther 2012, 2015), wherby their basis – examining different contexts of the emergence of the welfare state – loses its explanatory power against the backdrop of Europe-wide discourses.

In terms of content, it was possible to show the way in which public discourses and specialised discourses on employment support for disadvantaged young people, with reference to ideas of deficient young people and parents, legitimised law-making interventions and measures. In conjunction with this, the institutional analysis was able to describe the policy change and the changes run in the field of employment promotion in detail and on a small scale. It was shown that the changes in the area of employment promotion are gradually taking place in many small steps – in the direction of more activating and punitive policies. There are clear differences in the policies pursued by the various government coalitions. During the coalition of the social democratic SPÖ and the conservative ÖVP, a policy of social investment was pursued that was particularly influenced by social democratic positions, which led to the introduction of training guarantee and training obligation as well as to the measures established for their implementation. These interventions focus on young people, activate them especially within the framework of such (pedagogical) measures and channel their life courses. During the two coalitions of the conservative ÖVP and the far-right FPÖ, a policy strongly oriented towards the interests of companies was pursued, in which mainly financial rewards were distributed for the "offer" of apprenticeship places – i.e. the occupation of apprenticeship places. This policy not only favoured in-company training over other measures and emphasised the company as a quasi-pedagogical place of learning, but also made the labour force of apprentices more flexible.

The socio-political change in the promotion of employment for disadvantaged young people has also changed the framework conditions for social pedagogues, social workers and other professionals working in this field. They have to implement the more activation-oriented measures; their work increasingly takes place in coercive contexts.

In the professional discourse on the relationship between social policy and social work (e. g. Böhnisch et al. 2012; Bettinger 2012; Kessl/Otto 2009; Anhorn/Bettinger/Stehr 2008; Kaufmann 1973), the autonomy of social work and social pedagogy is reaffirmed or demanded from a theoretical perspective, e.g. by referring to the Code of Ethics of the *International Federation of Social Workers*. Correspondingly, at the theoretical level, the capability approach, which propagates the unconditional expansion of scope for action and orientation towards self-imposed goals, is becoming increasingly widespread as a guiding principle and theoretical underpinning of emancipatory approaches in social work.[70] However, social work in the field of youth employment developed diametrically in the context of social-investment, neoliberal, conservative and right-wing populist/extreme right social policies during the period under consideration. There are few opposing voices to these policies in the practice of employment promotion and social work as well as on the part of the professional associations. Social pedagogues and social workers "fight" only little

---

70 In this context, the capability approach of Amartya Sen and Martha Nussbaum deserves special attention. See: Otto/Schrödter 2007; Röh 2013; Otto et al. 2017; Leßmann/Otto/Ziegler 2011; Ziegler 2011.

(visibly) for the implementation of their professional demands. The largely depoliticised attitude of the social workers and social pedagogues working in this field is not reflected in their work (Benedikt/Huber 2022). This is worthy of attention insofar as the reflection of (socio-)political conditions and government activity as well as concrete interventions of social work – e.g. within the framework of policy practice – is not only of interest to the social workers and social pedagogues (Burzlaff/Eifler 2018), but has become an integral part of social work's professional self-image (Staub-Bernasconi 2018; Rieger 2016; Knecht/Schubert 2020: 318). In the field of youth employment promotion, however, this may also have to do with a field of activity in which the most diverse professional groups work together (and in some cases complement or even replace each other). As it is also common in comparable fields of work in Austria (cf. Sting 2015) the field of Youth Coaching, for example, is open to many professional groups. The employees are then trained in special courses or complete such courses before they are employed – which tends to stand in the way of professionalisation of social pedagogy and social work. In Austria a public discussion on the professional image and identity is underway, as is the professional associations' demand for a professional law. Considering that in Austria social pedagogy and social work do not manage to become an independent political weight and a power to shape practice in the field of employment promotion for young people, the question remains how the socio-political change affects the young people themselves.

An increased orientation of social and educational policies towards the social investment approach, neo liberal policies as well as right-wing populist/extreme right policies also changed the situation for the younger cohorts of young people (cf. Sting 2012). The years between 2000 and 2020 are characterised by a trend towards educational pathways with higher educational qualifications. The number of early school leavers was declining in the long term. In the context of the "educational lift" (cf. Beck 1986), that brings the whole society up, apprenticeship training continues to be an attractive goal for many young people. Against the background of a continuing decline in apprenticeship places, the training guarantee introduced in 2007 represented an increase in security in vocational training for young people.

With the introduction of compulsory training and education, a more obligatory, activating and punitive path was taken. While it become possible to take up auxiliary activities after compulsory schooling with the consequence of better formal educational opportunities, at the same time the youth period was channelled more strongly and the life courses or life trajectories were more strongly regulated. Intrinsically motivated action was replaced by extrinsically motivated action (Knecht 2016; Sandel 2012). This change must be seen against the background that disadvantaged young people in particular are implicitly or explicitly denied the ability to choose and pursue goals for themselves – instead, the focus is on "external control" (cf. Sting/Knecht 2022;

Sandel 2012). In addition to these changes, which are the result of the social investment policies of the SPÖ-ÖVP coalition, the changes of the ÖVP-FPÖ coalitions that flexibilise the labour market also have an impact on young people. While the various coalitions have each claimed to have improved the apprenticeship situation for young people, the increased pressure on them means that they are in danger of having to accept arbitrary jobs or apprenticeships and are thus forced into apprenticeships that do not correspond to their actual or long-term needs and interests (Knecht/Atzmüller 2019, cf. for general labour market policy also: Scherschel/Streckeisen/Krenn 2012; Pelizzari 2009). As discussed above, this shows a contradiction to the FPÖ's claim to do something for "the little/normal people", which becomes particularly visible through the separate analysis of discourses and institutions. The analysis of the situation and regulations regarding asylum-seeking young people (exclusion from education guarantee and obligation as well as inclusion or exclusion from the apprenticeship market) furthermore points to a policy of exclusion that was also pursued by the SPÖ-ÖVP coalition, but was enforced to an even greater extent by the ÖVP-FPÖ coalitions. For professionals working in the field of care and counselling of asylum-seeking young people, this means that their work is characterised by a lack of administration and can only have a limited effect on shaping their lives (see above).

Beyond the issue of exclusion of asylum-seeking young people, the activating policies in employment promotion also stand in the way of participatory measures or participative procedures in measures. The implementation of a social investment approach leads to narrowing the understanding of education down to an optimisation of employability (see above).

Social pedagogical increasingly takes place in labour market policy settings. Among others, the coalitions of right-wing parties, which particularly focused on subsidising companies, did not pursue strengthening youth participation. This also corresponds to analyses of right-wing populist/extreme right policies in other policy areas and countries, which see these policies favouring an authoritarian style (see e.g. Mudde and Rovira Kaltwasser 2019; Szelewa and Polakowski 2020), which is in stark contrast to the participation of young people and the consideration of the needs of different groups of disadvantaged young people.

In search of alternative ways, a broader spectrum of resources could be considered to support the development of young people (including psychological/mental and monetary resources). Educational opportunities could be designed in a more accessible and less segregated way and training (including vocational education and training) could be offered independently of the age of the person. A broad concept of education must emphasise human development potential over employability and thus postulate its voluntary nature (see for a broad concept of education e.g.: Sting 2018, 2022).

If the right to education were universalised, life courses could be better aligned with individual needs and dirigiste control and economic pressure could be minimised. Education could be seen more as an important part of democracy politics. In this context, it could be exciting for young people to discuss the importance of politics, especially with reference to the problem of finding a profession, including (apprenticeship) jobs, which is of acute concern to them at this age. Political vocational education and training could provide information on topics such as co-determination and opportunities for participation in the world of work as well as on the social conditionality and significance of work and unemployment, instead of – as proposed by the EU Youth Strategy – dealing solely with controversial concepts of talent and leading young people towards entrepreneurship. However, the analysis carried out shows that several current trends make the implementation of such alternatives increasingly unlikely.

8 Tabels

Table 1: Ratios of educational attainment and early school leavers by gender

Figures in percent	Educational attainment (according to ISCED 11) of 25 to 34-year-olds			Early school leavers (completion below upper secondary level) among 18 to 24-year-olds		
Year	Below upper secondary level (older ESL)	Upper secondary and post-secondary, non-tertiary	Tertiary level (levels 5–8)	Lower secondary level II	Quota of girls	Quota of boys
1995	21.1	70.1	8.8	13.6	17.3	9.9
1996	19.9	71.0	9.1	12.1	14.9	9.2
1997	17.0	73.7	9.3	10.8	12.5	9.0
1998	16.0	75.5	8.5	n.d.	n.d.	n.d.
1999	16.0	68.4	15.6	10.7	11.9	9.6
2000	(u)	(u)	(u)	10.2	10.7	9.6
2001	(u)	(u)	(u)	10.2	10.7	9.7
2002	(u)	(u)	(u)	9.5	10.2	8.7
2003	(u)	(u)	(u)	9.0	9.8	8.3
2004 (b)	13.0	66.9	20.1	9.8	9.1	10.5
2005	12.7	67.5	19.7	9.3	8.9	9.7
2006 (b)	13.0	68.0	19.0	10.0	9.8	10.3
2007	13.5	67.8	18.7	10.8	10.2	11.5
2008	12.5	68.3	19.2	10.2	9.9	10.4
2009	11.9	67.1	21.0	8.8	8.9	8.6
2010	12.2	67.1	20.7	8.3	8.3	8.4
2011	12.0	67.1	20.9	8.5	8.0	9.0
2012	11.6	65.6	22.8	7.8	7.6	8.0

Figures in percent	Educational attainment (according to ISCED 11) of 25 to 34-year-olds			Early school leavers (completion below upper secondary level) among 18 to 24-year-olds		
Year	Below upper secondary level (older ESL)	Upper secondary and post-secondary, non-tertiary	Tertiary level (levels 5–8)	Lower secondary level II	Quota of girls	Quota of boys
2013	10.9	64.1	24.9	7.5	7.1	7.9
2014 (b)	10.0	51.6	38.4	7.0	6.5	7.6
2015	10.0	51.4	38.6	7.3	6.8	7.8
2016	11.4	49.0	39.7	6.9	6.0	7.7
2017	11.5	48.2	40.3	7.4	5.8	9.0
2018	11.1	48.4	40.5	7.3	5.7	8.9
2019	10.6	47.8	41.6	7.8	6.1	9.5
2020	10.9	47.7	41.4	8.1	6.3	10.0

Data: Statistics Austria (2021a) and Eurostat (2021): edat_lfes_03, edat_lfes_14, 07-01-2022.
(u) = uncertain data; (b) = break in time series

Table 2: Unemployment rates by age and apprenticeship supply in Austria

Year	quota of unemployment (age 15–19)	quota of unemployment (age 20–24)	quota of unemp. (age 25–29)	quota of unemp. (25–29) – completion of no more than secondary level 1	early school leavers (age 18–24)	apprenticeship offer of companies (end of Dec.)	Training companies
1991	n.d.	n.d.	n.d.	n.d.	n.d.	141,099	41,676
1995	6.8	5.5	4.6	7.9	13.6	123,377	37,154
1996	7.3	6.6	5.6	8.9	12.1	119,932	36,685
1997	9.9	6.4	5.7	12.5	10.8	121,629	36,685
1998	10.0	6.2	4.8	10.9 (b)	-	123,596	39,540
1999	6.8	5.4	4.3	9.3 (u)	10.7	124,852	39,906
2000	6.8	6.0	4.4	7.8 (u)	10.2	124,015	39,302
2001	6.7	5.6	3.9	(u)	10.2	122,167	38,344
2002	7.3	7.1	5.1	8.8 (u)	9.5	119,300	37,216
2003	7.9	7.2	5.9	14.6 (u)	9.0	117,415	36,608
2004	14.9 (b)	10.7 (b)	6.1 (b)	17.7 (b)	9.8 (b)	117,431	36,139
2005	14.2 (b)	9.3 (b)	6.5 (b)	16.8 (b)	9.3	120,452	36,892
2006	12.7	8.2	6.2	16.8 (b)	10.0 (b)	123,047	37,783
2007	12.0 (b)	7.9 (b)	5.9 (b)	13.3 (b)	10.8	126,831	38,132
2008	11.5	6.8	5.1	14.5	10.2	128,233	37,983
2009	12.6	9.6	7.0	18.5	8.8	124,256	36,986
2010	11.1	8.5	6.5	17.4	8.3	120,437	36,004
2011	10.7	8.0	5.8	13.5	8.5	118,590	35,084
2012	10.5	8.8	6.5	18.5	7.8	115,707	33,732
2013	11.9	8.6	7.3	17.7	7.5	111,401	32,189
2014	11.4	9.8	7.2	19.1	7.0 (b)	105,861	30,570
2015	11.5	10.2	6.3	19.9	7.3	100,635	29,164
2016	14.1	10.0	7.0	20.7	6.9	97,706	28,204

Year	quota of un-employment (age 15–19)	quota of unemploy-ment (age 20–24)	quota of unemp. (age 25–29)	quota of unemp. (25–29) – completion of no more than secondary level 1	early school leavers (age 18–24)	apprenticeship offer of companies (end of Dec.)	Training companies
2017	12.5	8.7	6.4	23.3	7.4	97,512	27,792
2018	11.4	8.5	5.5	17.8	7.3	99,613	27,819
2019	10.9	7.6	5.0	13.8	7.8	101,689	27,844
2020	10.6	10.4	6.5	19.9	8.1		

Data: Eurostat (2021): yth_empl_090, edat_lfes_14, 15-08-2021 and ibid. Col. 6. and 7.: Dornmayr/Wieser/Mayerl 2012: 90; Dornmayr/Löffler 2020: 112; (u) = uncertain data, (b) = break in time series, "n.d." = no data

Table 3: Promotion/Subsidies for the youth active labour market policies (in € million)

Year	Total expenditure on youth [AMP][71]	Indirect corporate apprenticeship promotion[72]	Direct corporate apprenticeship job promotion[73]	Subsidies and grants from the AMS[74]	SCT (financed via AMS)[75]	SMS for NEBA (total)[76]	NEBA: Youth Coaching[77]	NEBA: Production schools (Ausbildungsfit)
1999	n.d.	40	-	n.d.	-	-	-	-
2000	n.d.	70	-	n.d.	-	-	-	-
2001	168,8	70	-	n.d.	-	-	-	-
2002	n.d.	150	-	n.d.	14,9	-	-	-
2003	n.d.	150	-	n.d.	22,9	-	-	-
2004	n.d.	133	-	225,9	38,8	-	-	-
2005	n.d.	146	-	207,4	38,9	-	-	-
2006	285	134	-	310,7	55,1	-	-	-
2007	n.d.	140	-	343,8	63,8	-	-	-
2008	561,8	153	-	372,2	86,3	-	-	-

71 Subsidies by Public Employment Service AMS including activating labour market policies for young people plus company-based apprenticeship subsidies. As of 2011, these numbers include social insurance contributions for activating benefits from unemployment insurance during the completion of a measure. In 2020, only the expenditure of active labour market policy (UG20) without the funds of the equalisation tax fund [ATF = UG21 BMSGPK] and without (Covid) short-time work are listed in the table.
72 Indirect promotion of apprenticeships through tax relief according to §108f Income Tax Act (EStG) 1988 as per promotion reports.
73 Company-based apprenticeship subsidies through apprenticeship subsidies (incl. administration) according to §19c Vocational Training Act in conjunction with §13e IESG – funds from the IEF according to subsidy reports.
74 The labour market promotion of the AMS includes the budget part for the so-called Active Labour Market Policy. The labour market promotion of the AMS is divided into three areas of intervention: the promotion of employment subsidies and measures, qualification subsidies and measures, and support subsidies and measures. Expenditure for the 'activating labour market policy', i.e. payments for the subsistence of participants during a measure, is not included. From 2020 on: without short-time work.
75 Supra-Company Training, incl. apprenticeship training, preparatory measures and accompanying measures.
76 Data from the BMSGPK, Department IV/A/6, data status as of 1st of Feb. 2022.
77 Figures according to the annual reports of youth coaching, production schools and NEBA.

Year	Total expenditure on youth [AMP][71]	Indirect corporate apprenticeship promotion[72]	Direct corporate apprenticeship job promotion[73]	Subsidies and grants from the AMS[74]	SCT (financed via AMS)[75]	SMS for NEBA (total)[76]	NEBA: Youth Coaching[77]	NEBA: Production schools (Ausbildungsfit)
2009	603,2	124	63,0+7,6	400,8	100,1		-	-
2010	n.d.	90	153,3+10,0	386,8	116,0		-	-
2011	686,3	-	153,8+5,6	382,0	148,4		-	-
2012	672,2	-	158,2+4,3	353,1	123,7		n.d.	-
2013	713,8	-	157,2+4,9	363,9	116,6		25	-
2014	773,4	-	159,0+6,7	384.8	126.4		26	n.d.
2015	792.1	-	142.4+6.2	401.2	154.1		25.9	18.9
2016	839.0	-	158.3+6.2	426.0	170.6		27.5	26.5
2017	867.0	-	156.3–6.5	445.0	174.7	116.6	33.0	31.5
2018	933.0	-	195.8+7.0	453.3	196.3	136.6	38.9	41.5
2019	925.9	-	221.4+7.5	415.5	177.9	149.3	44.4	46.1
2020	823.1	-	211.8+8.0	399.4	169.5	161.5		

I would like to thank Kai Hartig at the Federal Ministry of Labour for the data in columns 1, 2 and 5.

Table 4: Number of apprentices and participants in measures

Year	Company offer of apprenticeship places (end of Dec. each year)[78]	Supported by PES "AMS" subsidies and grants (15–19)[79]	Supported by PES "AMS" subsidies and grants (20–24)	measure SCT (number of persons promoted)[80]	NEBA: Youth Coaching[81]	NEBA: Production schools/ "Ausbildungsfit"[81]
1991	141,099					
1995	123,377					
1996	119,932					
1997	121,629					
1998	123,596					
1999	124,852	n.d.	n.d.			
2000	124,015	n.d.	n.d.			
2001	122,167	n.d.	n.d.			
2002	119,300	n.d.	n.d.			
2003	117,415	n.d.	n.d.			
2004	117,431	n.d.	n.d.			
2005	120,452	n.d.	n.d.			
2006	123,047	n.d.	n.d.			
2007	126,831	78,425	46,926			
2008	128,233	75,660	47,270			

78 Realised "in-company apprenticeship places" according to data from the BMA as of January 2022. See additionally Dornmayr/Wieser/Mayerl 2012: 90; Dornmayr/Löffler 2020: S. 112.
79 Number of persons supported by the Public Employment Service AMS (in 2020 without (Covid) short-time work) according to Federal Ministry of Employment (BMA) data from 2020. Supplementary data in square brackets.
80 AMS DWH, number of persons per year incl. preparatory and accompanying measures of supra-company training (SCT) (data status: 5th of January 2022).
81 According to the annual reports of Youth Coaching, production school ("Ausbildungsfit") and NEBA (ongoing from 2017).

Year	Company offer of apprenticeship places (end of Dec. each year)[78]	Supported by PES "AMS" subsidies and grants (15–19)[79]	Supported by PES "AMS" subsidies and grants (20–24)	measure SCT (number of persons promoted)[80]	NEBA: Youth Coaching[81]	NEBA: Production schools/ "Ausbildungsfit"[81]
2009	124,256	72,570	64,894			
2010	120,437	65,297	62,976			
2011	118,590	54,934	53,472			
2012	115,707	53,838	56,962	13,211		
2013	111,401	55,244	64,163	18,627	27,546	
2014	105,816	55,358	65,745	18,388	27,570	1,268
2015	100,635	53,779	64,515	19,949	39,361	2,207
2016	97,706	53,882	65,674	20,807	45,132	3,187
2017	97,512	56,068	64,407	23,761	51,529	4,130
2018	99,613	56,116	57,391	23,431	55,702	4,769
2019	101,689	54,271	51,394	23,541	60,082	5,196
2020	101,176	51,135 [105,445]	48,846 [168,285]	21,954		

I would like to thank Kai Hartig at the Federal Ministry of Labour for the data in columns 2 and 3.

9 References

Acconcia, Giuseppe/Atzmüller, Roland/Baillergeau, Evelyne/Belda-Miquel, Sergio/... Knecht, Alban et al. (2017): Improving the quality of life of disadvantaged young people in Europe. In: Otto, Hans-Uwe/Egdell, Valerie/Bonvin, Jean-Michel/Atzmüller, Roland (eds.): Empowering Young People in Disempowering Times. Cheltenham, UK, Northhampton, MA: Edward Elgar, pp. 251–261.

Afonso, Alexandre (2015): Choosing whom to betray: populist right-wing parties, welfare state reforms and the trade-off between office and votes. In: European Political Science Review 7, 2, pp. 271–292.

AG Jugendforschung (2018): Jugendcoaching – Ein Beratungsangebot der Beschäftigungsförderung für benachteiligte Jugendliche in Österreich. Unpublished research report of a seminar at Johannes Kepler University, Linz, 2017/18.

Alkire, Sabina/Foster, James E./Seth, Suman/Santos, Maria Emma/Roche, José Manuel/Ballón, Paola (2015): Multidimensional poverty measurement and analysis. Oxford: Oxford University Press.

Allmendinger, Jutta/Leibfried, Stephan (2003): Education and the welfare state: The four Worlds of Competence Production. In: Journal of European Social Policy 13, 1, pp. 63–81.

Althusser, Louis (1977): Ideologie und ideologische Staatsapparate. Hamburg: VSA.

Am Rand (2022): gleich ≠ gleich: Diskriminierung im Schulalltag. https://www.amrand.at/post/diskriminierung-im-schulalltag [access: 08-12-2022].

AMS Austria (2013): Bundesrichtlinie zur Durchführung der Überbetrieblichen (Integrativen) Berufsausbildung (ÜBA, IBA) durch das AMS. GZ: BGS/AMF/0722/9906/2013; AMF/4-2013. Wien.

AMS Austria (2016): Geschäftsbericht 2015. Wien.

Andresen, Sabine (2010): Bildungsmotivation in bildungsfernen Gruppen und Schichten. In: Quenzel, Gudrun/Hurrelmann, Klaus (eds.): Bildungsverlierer. Neue Ungleichheiten. Wiesbaden: VS, pp. 499–516.

Anhorn, Roland/Bettinger, Frank/Stehr, Johannes (2008): Sozialer Ausschluss und soziale Arbeit. Positionsbestimmungen einer kritischen Theorie und Praxis sozialer Arbeit. Perspektiven kritischer Sozialer Arbeit. Wiesbaden: VS. 2nd ed.

Antonovsky, Aaron (1987): Unraveling the mystery of health. How People Manage Stress and Stay Well. Jossey-Bass social and behavioral science series. San Francisco, Calif.: Jossey-Bass.

APA OTS (2018a): FPÖ-Gudenus: "Neues Mindestsicherungsmodell bringt Fairness für Österreicher". APA-OTS-Meldung, 29-01-2018. https://www.ots.at/presseaussendung/OTS_20181129_OTS0083/fpoe-gudenus-neues-mindestsicherungsmodell-bringt-fairness-fuer-oesterreicher [access: 20-01-2020].

APA OTS (2018b): Landesrat Waldhäusl: "Mindestsicherung NEU" stellt Hilfestellung für in Notlage geratene Österreicher langfristig sicher. APA-OTS-Meldung vom 28.11.2018. Topf kann von integrationsunwilligen Massenzuwanderern nicht mehr haltlos geplündert werden. https://www.ots.at/presseaussendung/OTS_20181128_OTS0141/landesrat-waldhaeusl-mindestsicherung-neu-stellt-hilfestellung-fuer-in-notlage-geratene-oesterreicher-langfristig-sicher [access: 20-01-2020].

APA OTS (2018c): Wöginger/Rosenkranz: Wir machen Schluss mit der Zuwanderung ins Sozialsystem. APA-OTS-Meldung vom 30-11-2018. https://www.ots.at/presseaussendung/OTS_20181130_OTS0159/woegingerrosenkranz-wir-machen-schluss-mit-der-zuwanderung-ins-sozialsystem [access: 20-01-2020].

Atzmüller, Roland (2009): Aktivierung statt Vollbeschäftigung. Die Entwicklung der Arbeitsmarktpolitik in Österreich. In: Hermann, Christoph/Atzmüller, Roland (eds.): Die Dynamik des "österreichischen Modells". FORBA-Forschung, Vol. 4. Berlin: edition sigma, pp. 135–186.

Atzmüller, Roland (2014): Aktivierung der Arbeit im Workfare-Staat. Arbeitsmarkt und Ausbildung nach dem Fordismus. Münster: Westfälisches Dampfboot.

Atzmüller, Roland (2022): Renationalisierung der Sozialpolitik. In: Betzelt, Sigrid/Fehmel, Thilo (eds.): Deformation oder Transformation? Analysen zum wohlfahrtsstaatlichen Wandel. Wiesbaden: VS, pp. 25–47.

Atzmüller, Roland/Décieux, Fabienne/Knecht, Alban (2019): Transforming Children and Adolescents in Human Capital. Changes of Youth Policies in Post-Crisis Austria. In: Grimm, Marc/Ertugrul, Baris/Bauer, Ullrich (eds.): Children and Adolescents in Times of Crises in Europe. Children's Well-Being: Indicators and Research, Vol. 20, pp. 107–123.

Atzmüller, Roland/Knecht, Alban (2016a): Neoliberale Transformation der österreichischen Beschäftigungspolitik für Jugendliche. In: SWS-Rundschau 56, 1, pp. 112–132.

Atzmüller, Roland/Knecht, Alban (2016b): Zusammenhänge von Bildungs- und Sozialpolitik. In: Grüne Bildungswerkstatt (ed.): Solidarisch und selbstbestimmt. Die neuen Chancen des Sozialstaats. Wien: Eigenverlag, pp. 30–33.

Atzmüller, Roland/Knecht, Alban (2017a): Die Legitimation von Aktivierung und social investment und die Pathologisierung jugendlicher Subjektivität. Ausbildungspolitik und Beschäftigungsförderung für 'benachteiligte' Jugendliche in der Krise. In: Aulenbacher, Brigitte/Dammayr, Maria/Dörre, Klaus/Menz, Wolfgang/ Riegraf, Birgit/Wolf, Harald (eds.): Leistung und Gerechtigkeit. Das umstrittene Versprechen des Kapitalismus. Arbeitsgesellschaft im Wandel. Weinheim und Basel: Beltz Juventa, pp. 118–135.

Atzmüller, Roland/Knecht, Alban (2017b): Vocational training in the framework of the 'Austrian Training Guarantee'. In: Otto, Hans-Uwe/Egdell, Valerie/Bonvin, Jean-Michel/Atzmüller, Roland (eds.): Empowering Young People in Disempowering Times. Fighting Inequality Through Capability Oriented Policy. Cheltenham, UK, Northhampton, MA: Edward Elgar, pp. 115–128.

Atzmüller, Roland/Knecht, Alban (2018): Transformation of Work and Welfare – Apprentices under Neoliberalism. In: Social Work & Society 16, 2.

Atzmüller, Roland/Knecht, Alban/Bodenstein, Michael (2020): Punishing the Poor and Fighting "Immigration into the Social System" – Welfare Reforms by the Conservative and Far-right Government in Austria 2017–2019. In: Zeitschrift für Sozialreform/Journal for Social Policy Research 66, 4, 525–522.

Atzmüller, Roland/Krenn, Manfred/Papouschek, Ulrike (2012): Innere Aushöhlung und Fragmentierung des österreichischen Modells: Zur Entwicklung von Arbeitslosigkeit, prekärer Beschäftigung und Arbeitsmarktpolitik. In: Scherschel, Karin/Streckeisen, Peter/Krenn, Manfred (eds.): Neue Prekarität. Die Folgen aktivierender Arbeitsmarktpolitik – Europäische Länder im Vergleich. Labour Studies, Vol. 2. Frankfurt/M., New York: Campus, pp. 75–110.

Austrian Government (2000): Bundesregierung: Zukunft im Herzen Europas: Österreich neu regieren. Das Regierungsprogramm. Wien.
Austrian National Assembly (1998): Parlamentskorrespondenz Nr. 283, 30-04-1998. Weitere Punkte des Budetbegleitgesetzes 1998. Wien.
Austrian National Assembly (2002): Stenographisches Protokoll. 104. Sitzung des Nationalrates der Republik Österreich. Donnerstag, 23-05-2002. Wien.
Austrian National Assembly (2010): Vereinbarung zwischen dem Bund und den Ländern gemäß Art. 15a B-VG über eine bundesweite Bedarfsorientierte Mindestsicherung.
Austrian National Assembly (2013): Stenographisches Protokoll, 194. Sitzung des Nationalrates der Republik Österreich, 21-03-2013. Wien.
Austrian National Assembly (2016): Parlamentskorrespondenz Nr. 411, 27-04-2016: Recht auf Asylverfahren kann künftig zeitweilig eingeschränkt werden. Parlamentskorrespondenz, 411. Wien.
Austrian National Assembly (2017a): Ministerialentwurf – Erläuterungen zum Integrationsjahrgesetz. 291/ME XXV. GP. Wien.
Austrian National Assembly (2017b): Parlamentskorrespondenz Nr. 817 vom 28-06-2017. Fremdenrechtspaket bringt Gebietsbeschränkungen für Flüchtlinge und Beugehaft. Wien.
Austrian National Assembly (2019): Erläuterungen. 514 der Beilagen XXVI. GP – Regierungsvorlage. Wien. https://www.parlament.gv.at/dokument/XXVI/I/514/fname_740754.pdf [access: 21-01-2020].
Austrian National Assembly (2020a): Bundesgesetz betreffend Grundsätze für die Sozialhilfe (Sozialhilfe-Grundsatzgesetz) BGBl. I Nr. 41/2019
Austrian National Assembly (2020b): Entschließungsantrag der Abgeordneten Dr. Stephanie Krisper, Kolleginnen und Kollegen betreffend Angleichung der Tagessätze in der Grundversorgung für unbegleitete minderjährig Geflüchtete. 768/A(E) XXXVII. GP. Wien.
Bacher, Johann/Braun, Julius/Burtscher-Mathis, Simon/Dlabaja, Cornelia (2014): Unterstützung der arbeitsmarktpolitischen Zielgruppe "NEET". Sozialpolitische Studienreihe, Vol. 17. Wien.
Badelt, Christoph/Böheim, René/Eppel, Rainer/Fink, Marian/Horvath, Thomas/Huemer, Ulrike/Mahringer, Helmut (2019): Szenarien der Gestaltung von Existenzsicherungsleistungen der Arbeitslosenversicherung. Wien.
Bakic, Josef/Diebäcker, Marc/Hammer, Elisabeth (2008): Die Ökonomisierung Sozialer Arbeit in Österreich. In: Sozial Extra 32, 1–2, pp. 52–55.
Bareis, Ellen (2020): Soziale Ausschließung und die Grenzen der repräsentativen Demokratie. Die Perspektive from below. In: Appel, Margit/Fabris, Verena/Knecht, Alban et al. (eds.): Stimmen gegen Armut. Weil soziale Ungleichheit und Ausgrenzung die Demokratie gefährden. Norderstedt: BoD-Verlag, pp. 27–38.
Bareis, Ellen/Cremer-Schäfer, Helga (2013): Empirische Alltagsforschung als Kritik Grundlagen der Forschungsperspektive der "Wohlfahrtsproduktion von unten". In: Graßhoff, Gunther (ed.): Adressaten, Nutzer, Agency. Akteursbezogene Forschungsperspektiven in der Sozialen Arbeit. Wiesbaden: Springer VS, pp. 139–159.
Bareis, Ellen/Wagner, Thomas (eds.) (2015): Politik mit der Armut. Europäische Sozialpolitik und Wohlfahrtsproduktion "von unten". Münster: Westfälisches Dampfboot.

Bauer, Fritz/Kainz, Gudrun (2007): Benachteiligung von Kindern mit Migrationshintergrund beim Bildungszugang. In: WISO 30, 4, pp. 17–64.
Bauer, Gernot (2021): ÖVP-Parteitag: Der Reiz des Simplen. In: Profil. https://www.profil.at/oesterreich/oevp-parteitag-der-reiz-des-simplen/401484619 [Zugriff: 08.10.2023]
Baumgartner, Josef/Fink, Marian/Kaniovski, Serguei/Rocha-Akis, Silvia (2018): Gesamtwirtschaftliche Auswirkungen der Einführung des Familienbonus Plus und des Kindermehrbetrags. In: WIFO-Monatsberichte 91, 10, pp. 745–755.
Becker, Joachim (2023): Rechte Sozialpolitik zwischen Neoliberalismus und Nationalkonservatismus in Zentralosteuropa: Ungarn und Polen. In: Atzmüller, Roland/Décieux, Fabienne/Ferschli, Benjamin (eds.): Ambivalenzen in der Transformation von Sozialpolitik und Wohlfahrtsstaat. Soziale Arbeit, Care, Rechtspopulimus und Migration. Weinheim: Beltz Juventa.
Becker, Rolf/Lauterbach, Wolfgang (eds.) (2016): Bildung als Privileg? Erklärungen und Befunde zu den Ursachen der Bildungsgleichheit. Wiesbaden: Springer VS. 5th ed.
Benedikt, Marina/Huber, Sabrina (2022): Eine Erhebung zur Haltung von Fachkräften zu politischem Handeln der Sozialen Arbeit. Klagenfurt: Unpublished manuscript.
Bettinger, Frank (2012): Soziale Arbeit und Sozialpolitik. In: Thole, Werner (ed.): Grundriss Soziale Arbeit. Ein einführendes Handbuch. Wiesbaden: VS. 4th ed., pp. 345–354.
Betzelt, Sigrid (2019): Autoritäre Tendenzen in der Sozialpolitik? https://www.weiterdenken.de/de/2019/07/15/autoritaere-tendenzen-der-sozialpolitik [access: 18-02-2022].
Betzelt, Sigrid/Bothfeld, Silke (2014): Autonomie – ein neues Leitbild einer modernen Arbeitsmarktpolitik. Bonn.
Betzelt, Sigrid/Fehmel, Thilo (eds.) (2022): Deformation oder Transformation? Analysen zum wohlfahrtsstaatlichen Wandel. Wiesbaden: VS.
Biffl, Gudrun/Skrivanek, Isabella (2014): Jugendliche mit Migrationshintergrund in der Lehre. Strukturen, Barrieren, Potentiale. Krems.
Biskamp, Floris (2019): Six theories and six strategies concerning right-wing populism. In: Bevelander, Pieter/Wodak, Ruth (eds.): Europe at the Crossroads. Confronting Populist, Nationalist, and Global Challenges. Nordic Academic Press, pp. 93–112.
Bissuti, Romeo/Scambor, Elli/Scambor, Christian/Siegel, Eberhard/Pljevaljcic, Predag/Zingerle, Markus (2013): Bedarfsanalyse unterstützender Maßnahmen von sozial benachteiligten männlichen Jugendlichen an der Schnittstelle Ausbildung und Erwerbsarbeit. Wien.
Blommaert, Jan/Bulcaen, Chris (2000): Critical Discourse Analysis. In: Annual Review of Anthropology 29, pp. 447–466.
Blum, Sonja/Schubert, Klaus (2018): Politikfeldanalyse. Wiesbaden: Springer VS. 3rd ed.
BMAFJ (2016): Fragen und Antworten zur Ausbildung bis 18. Wien.
BMASK (2013a): Aktive Arbeitsmarktpolitik in Österreich 1994–2013. Wien.
BMASK (2013b): Arbeitsmarktpolitik im Jahr 2012. Wien.
BMASK (2015a): Auftaktveranstaltung: "AusBildung bis 18" – alle gemeinsam für die Zukunft unserer Jugend. Pressemitteilung OTS0059, 30-01-2015. Wien.
BMASK (2015b): Jugend und Arbeit in Österreich. Berichtsjahr 2014/2015. Wien.
BMASK (2020): Jugend und Arbeit in Österreich. Berichtsjahr 2019/2020. Wien.

BMDW (2018): Schramböck: Paket zur Lehrlingsförderung weiterer Schritt zur Bekämpfung des Fachkräftemangels. Pressemeldung des Bundesministeriums für Digitalisierung und Wirtschaft, 28-11-2018. Wien: APA.

BMSGPK (2019): AusBildung bis 18 – Studie zur Implementierung und Umsetzung des Ausbildungspflichtgesetzes. Wissenschaftlich belegter, vielfältiger Nutzen der AusBildung bis 18. Wien.

Bodenstein, Michael/Knecht, Alban (2017): Existentielles Warten. Bildungswege und Alltagsstrategien jugendlicher Asylsuchender. In: Asyl Aktuell. Zeitschrift der Asylkoordination Österreich, 4, pp. 24–27.

Boeckh, Jürgen/Benz, Benjamin/Huster, Ernst-Ulrich/Schütte, Johannes D. (2015a): Aktuelle sozialpolitische Leitbilder. In: Informationen zur politischen Bildung, 327, pp. 30–35.

Boeckh, Jürgen/Benz, Benjamin/Huster, Ernst-Ulrich/Schütte, Johannes D. (2015b): Sozialpolitische Akteure und Prozesse im Mehrebenensystem. In: Informationen zur politischen Bildung, 54-67.

Böhnisch, Lothar/Lösch, Christian (1973): Das Handlungsverständnis des Sozialarbeiters und seine institutionelle Determination. Zur gegenwärtigen Diskussion über den politisch-sozialen Standort des Sozialarbeiters. In: Otto, Hans-Uwe/Schneider, Siegfried (eds.): Gesellschaftliche Perspektiven der Sozialarbeit. Zweiter Halbband. Neuwied, Berlin: Luchterhand, pp. 21–40.

Böhnisch, Lothar/Schröer, Wolfgang/Arnold, Helmut/Schefold, Werner/Keupp, Heiner/Lorenz, Walter (2012): Sozialpolitik und Soziale Arbeit. Eine Einführung. Weinheim, Basel: Beltz Juventa.

Bohrn Mena, Veronika (2020): Die neue ArbeiterInnenklasse. Menschen in prekären Verhältnissen. Wien: ÖGB Verlag. 3rd ed.

Bommes, Michael/Scherr, Albert (2000): Soziale Arbeit, sekundäre Ordnungsbildung und die Kommunikation unspezifischer Hilfsbedürftigkeit. In: Merten, Roland (ed.): Systemtheorie sozialer Arbeit. Neue Ansätze und veränderte Perspektiven. Lehrtexte Erziehung. Opladen: Leske + Budrich, pp. 67–86.

Bonavida, Iris (2018): Asyl auf (etwas mehr) Zeit. In: Die Presse, 11-02-2018. https://www.diepresse.com/5369177/asyl-auf-etwas-mehr-zeit [access: 11-10-23]

Bonvalot, Michael (2017): Die FPÖ – Partei der Reichen. Kritik & Utopie. Wien: mandelbaum.

Bonvin, Jean-Michel/Galster, Déborah (2010): Making them Employable or Capable? Social Integration Policies at a Crossroads. In: Otto, Hans-Uwe/Ziegler, Holger (eds.): Education, Welfare and the Capabilities Approach. A European Perspective. Opladen, Farmington Hills: Budrich, pp. 71–84.

Borrelli, Lisa Marie/Bochsler, Yann (2020): Editorial: Governing the Poor – Migration and Poverty. In: Zeitschrift für Sozialreform 66, 4, pp. 363–385.

Bothfeld, Silke (2017): Autonomie – ein Kernbegriff moderner Sozialstaatlichkeit. In: Zeitschrift für Sozialreform/Journal for Social Policy Research 63, 3, pp. 355–387.

Bourdieu, Pierre (1984): Distinction: A Social Critic of the Judgement of Taste. Cambridge, Massachusetts: Harvard University Press.

Bourdieu, Pierre (1992): Ökonomisches Kapital – Kulturelles Kapital – Soziales Kapital. In: Bourdieu, Pierre (ed.): Die verborgenen Mechanismen der Macht. Schriften zu Politik & Kultur, Vol. 1. Hamburg: VSA, pp. 49–79.

Bröckling, Ulrich (2007): Das unternehmerische Selbst. Soziologie einer Subjektivierungsform. Frankfurt/M.: Suhrkamp.

Bröckling, Ulrich/Krasmann, Susanne/Lemke, Thomas (eds.) (2000): Gouvernementalität der Gegenwart. Studien zur Ökonomisierung des Sozialen. Frankfurt/M.: Suhrkamp.
Bronfenbrenner, Urie (1981): Die Ökologie der menschlichen Entwicklung. Stuttgart: Klett-Cotta.
Bruff, Ian (2013): The Rise of Authoritarian Neoliberalism. In: Rethinking Marxism 26, 1, pp. 113–129.
Buchwald, Petra/Schwarzer, Christine/Hobfoll, Stevan E. (eds.) (2004): Stress gemeinsam bewältigen – Ressourcenmanagement und multiaxiales Coping. Göttingen: Hogrefe.
Budget Service of the Parliament of the Republic of Austria (2018): Anfragebeantwortung des Budgetdienstes. Verteilungswirkung des Familienbonus und alternativer Förderungsmodelle. Wien.
Bührmann, Andrea D./Schneider, Werner (2008): Vom Diskurs zum Dispositiv. Eine Einführung in die Dispositivanalyse. Sozialtheorie Intro. Bielefeld: transcript.
Bundeskanzleramt (2021): Österreichische Jugendstrategie. Fortschrittsbericht 2021. Wien.
Burzlaff, Miriam/Eifler, N. (2018): Kritisch intervenieren!? Über Selbstverständnisse, Kritik und Politik Sozialer Arbeit. In: Prasad, Nivedita (ed.): Soziale Arbeit mit Geflüchteten. Rassismuskritisch, professionell, menschenrechtsorientiert. UTB Soziale Arbeit, Vol. 4851. Opladen, Toronto: Verlag Barbara Budrich, pp. 345–365.
Büschken, Michael (2017): Soziale Arbeit unter den Bedingungen des »aktivierenden Sozialstaates«. Weinheim: Beltz.
Butterwegge, Christoph (2018): Demografie als Mittel rechtspopulistischer Demagogie. Familienfundamentalismus und Bevölkerungspolitik der AfD. Familienfundamentalismus und Bevölkerungspolitik der AfD. In: Sozialismus, 10, pp. 19–23.
Butterwegge, Christoph (2021): Die überforderte Bildung. Bildung schützt nicht wirksam vor Armut und nützt auch wenig im Kampf gegen soziale Ungleichheit. In: Schulheft, 184, pp. 68–78.
Butterwegge, Christoph/Lösch, Bettina/Ptak, Ralf (eds.) (2008): Kritik des Neoliberalismus. Wiesbaden: VS. 2nd ed.
Buttner, Peter/Knecht, Alban (2009): Wege der Ressourcendiagnostik in der Sozialen Arbeit – ein ressourcentheoretisch fundierter Überblick. In: Pantucek, Peter/Röh, Dieter (eds.): Perspektiven Sozialer Diagnostik. Über den Stand der Entwicklung von Verfahren und Standards. Wien: LIT, pp. 99–110.
Buxbaum, Adi (2014): Perspektiven für Sozialen Fortschritt. Sozialinvestitionen haben eine Mehrfachdividende. Sozialpolitik in Diskussion. Wien.
Cantillon, Bea (2011): The paradox of the social investment state: growth, employment and poverty in the Lisbon era. In: Journal of European Social Policy 21, 5, pp. 432–449.
Chamber of Labour Upper Austria (2018): Das neue Arbeitszeitrecht. Linz.
Clark, Zoë/Ziegler, Holger (2016): Jugend, Capabilities und das Problem der Pädagogik. In: Becker, Ulrike/Friedrichs, Henrike/Gross, Friederike von/Kaiser, Sabine (eds.): Ent-Grenztes Heranwachsen. Wiesbaden: Springer VS, pp. 219–232.
Dahmen, Stephan/Bonvin, Jean-Michel/Beuret, Benoit (2017): The dynamics of youth policies in Switzerland: between particpation and activation. In: Otto, Hans-Uwe/ Egdell, Valerie/Bonvin, Jean-Michel/Atzmüller, Roland (eds.): Empowering

Young People in Disempowering Times. Fighting Inequality Through Capability Oriented Policy. Cheltenham, UK, Northhampton, MA: Edward Elgar, pp. 144–159.

Dallinger, Ursula/Fückel, Sebastian (2014): Politische Grundlagen und Folgen von Dualisierungsprozessen: Eine politische Ökonomie der Hartz-Reformen. In: WSI-Mitteilungen 67, 3, pp. 182–191.

Dehnbostel, Peter (2020): Der Betrieb als Lernort. In: Arnold, Rolf/Lipsmeier, Antonius/Rohs, Matthias (ed.): Handbuch Berufsbildung. Wiesbaden: Springer VS, pp. 1–17.

Der Standard (2018a): Mehrheit laut Umfrage gegen Abschiebung von Lehrlingen. In: Der Standard, 21-07-2018. https://www.derstandard.at/story/2000083887906/mehrheit-laut-umfrage-gegen-abschiebung-von-lehrlingen [access: 30-08-2023].

Der Standard (2018b): Regionalisierte Mangelberufsliste soll Anfang 2019 kommen. In: Der Standard, 12-09-2018. https://www.derstandard.at/story/2000087208285/regionalisierte-mangelberuf-liste-soll-anfang-2019-kommen [access: 30-08-2023].

Der Standard (2018c): ÖVP Vorarlberg fordert Rot-Weiß-Rot-Card für Asylwerber nach Lehre. Der Antrag für Karte soll künftig auch in Österreich gestellt werden können. In: Der Standard, 28-9-2018. https://www.derstandard.at/story/2000088280879/oevp-vorarlberg-fordert-rot-weiss-rot-card-fuer-asylwerber-mit [access: 30-08-2023].

Der Standard (2021): Kocher will "strenge Praxis" bei Asylwerbern am Arbeitsmarkt möglichst beibehalten. In: Der Standard, 15-07-2021. https://www.derstandard.at/story/2000128198607/kocher-will-strenge-praxis-bei-asylwerbern-moeglichst-beibehalten [access: 30-08-2023].

Der Standard (2022): FPÖ-Landesrat Waldhäusl wegen Flüchtlingsquartiers Drasenhofen vor Gericht. In: Der Standard, 02.02. https://www.derstand ard.at/jetzt/livebericht/2000133035529/prozess-gegen-fpoe-walshaeusl-wegen-fluechtlingsquartiers-startet [access: 30-08-2023].

Diaz-Bone, Rainer (2018): Foucaultsche Diskursanalyse und Ungleichheitsforschung. In: Zeitschrift für Qualitative Forschung 19, 1+2, pp. 47–61.

Die Presse (2016): Strache: Flüchtlingswelle ist "feindliche Landnahme". In: Die Presse 2016.

Die Presse (2018a): Van der Bellen zur Mindestsicherung: Pläne der Regierung "echtes Problem". In: Die Presse.

Die Presse (2018b): Immer mehr ÖVP-Vertreter gegen Abschiebung von Lehrlingen. 25-08-2018. In: Die Presse. https://www.diepresse.com/5485130/immer-mehr-oevp-vertreter-gegen-abschiebung-von-lehrlingen [access: 11-10-2023]

Die Presse (2018c): FPÖ will Zugang zur Lehre für Asylwerber wieder verbieten. In: Die Presse, 26-08-2018, Wien. https://www.diepresse.com/5485983/fpoe-will-zugang-zur-lehre-fuer-asylwerber-wieder-verbieten [access: 11-10-2023]

Die Presse (2018d): Arbeitsmarktservice streicht Großteil der Deutschkurse. In: Die Presse, 30-11-2018, Wien. https://www.diepresse.com/5538879/arbeitsmarktservice-streicht-grossteil-der-deutschkurse [access: 11-10-2023]

Die Presse (2020): VwGH hebt Abschiebung von Lehrling aus Vorarlberg auf. In: Die Presse, 27-02-2018, Wien. https://www.diepresse.com/5775712/vwgh-hebt-abschiebung-von-lehrling-aus-vorarlberg-auf [access: 11-10-2023]

Diebäcker, Marc/Hammer, Elisabeth (2009): Zur Rolle von Sozialer Arbeit im Staat. Skizzen aus regulationstheoretischer und Foucault'scher Perspektive. In: Kurswechsel, 3, pp. 11–25.

Diebäcker, Marc/Ranftler, Judith/Strahner, Tamara/Wolfgruber, Gudrun (2009a): Neoliberale Strategien und die Regulierung sozialer Organisationen im lokalen Staat. Politiken zur Depolitisierung und Deprofessionalisierung der Sozialen Arbeit – Teil I. In: soziales kapital, 3, pp. 1–20.

Diebäcker, Marc/Ranftler, Judith/Strahner, Tamara/Wolfgruber, Gudrun (2009b): Zeugnisse alltäglichen Leidens in sozialen Organisationen. Von der Ökonomisierung des Politischen zur Depolitisierung und Deprofessionalisierung der Sozialen Arbeit – Teil II. In: soziales kapital, 4, pp. 1–16.

Dommermuth, Lars (2008): Wege ins Erwachsenenalter in Europa. Italien, Westdeutschland und Schweden im Vergleich. Wiesbaden: VS.

Dornmayr, Helmut/Litschel, Veronika/Löffler, Roland (2016): Bericht zur Situation der Jugendbeschäftigung und Lehrlingsausbildung in Österreich 2014–2015.

Dornmayr, Helmut/Litschel, Veronika/Löffler, Roland (2017): Die Lehrstellenförderung des AMS im Fokus einer aktuellen Evaluierung: Zentrale Ergebnisse einer aktuellen Studie im Auftrag des AMS Österreich. AMS Info. Wien.

Dornmayr, Helmut/Löffler, Roland (2020): Bericht zur Situation der Jugendbeschäftigung und Lehrlingsausbildung in Österreich 2018–2019. Wien.

Dornmayr, Helmut/Nowak, Sabine (2017): Lehrlingsausbildung im Überblick 2017. Strukturdaten, Trends und Perspektiven. ibw-Forschungsbericht. Wien.

Dornmayr, Helmut/Nowak, Sabine (2019): Lehrlingsausbildung im Überblick 2019. Strukturdaten, Trends und Perspektiven. ibw-Forschungsbericht. Wien.

Dornmayr, Helmut/Petanovitsch, Alexander/Winkler, Birgit (2016): Kontext- und Implementationsanalyse der betrieblichen Lehrstellenförderung (gemäß §19c BAG). Teilbericht im Rahmen der ibw-öibf-Studie "Hintergrundanalyse zur Wirksamkeit der betrieblichen Lehrstellenförderung (gemäß §19c BAG)". Wien.

Dornmayr, Helmut/Wieser, Regine (2010): Bericht zur Situation der Lehrlingsbeschäftigung und Lehrlingsausbildung in Österreich 2008–2009. ibw-Forschungsbericht. Wien.

Dornmayr, Helmut/Wieser, Regine/Mayerl, Martin (2012): Bericht zur Situation der Jugendbeschäftigung und Lehrlingsausbildung in Österreich 2010–2011. Wien.

Dörre, Klaus/Scherschel, Karin/Booth, Melanie Booth/Haubner, Tine/Marquardsen, Kai/Schierhorn, Karen (2013): Bewährungsproben für die Unterschicht? Soziale Folgen aktivierender Arbeitsmarktpolitik. International labour studies. Frankfurt/M., New York: Campus.

Drilling, Matthias (2004): Young urban poor. Abstiegsprozesse in den Zentren der Sozialstaaten. Wiesbaden: VS.

Drljic, Dragana/Holzer, Petra (2017): Die Wohn- und Betreuungssituation von umF und fremduntergebrachten Jugendlichen. Masterarbeit. Graz: Universität Graz.

Düggeli, Albert (2009): Ressourcenförderung im Berufswahlunterricht. Interventionsstudie mit Lernenden der Sekundarstufe I, Niveau Grundanforderungen. Münster: Waxmann.

Dworkin, Ronald (2011): Was ist Gleichheit? Berlin: Suhrkamp.

Eberhard, Verena (2012): Der Übergang von der Schule in die Berufsausbildung. Ein ressourcentheoretisches Modee zur Erklärung der Übergangschancen von Ausbildungsstellenbewerbern. Bielefeld: wbv.

Ebert, Thomas (2015): Soziale Gerechtigkeit. Schriftenreihe, Vol. 1571. Bonn: Bundeszentrale für politische Bildung. 2nd ed.
Edelman, Murray J. (2005): Politik als Ritual. Die symbolische Funktion staatlicher Institutionen und politischen Handelns. Frankfurt/M., New York: Campus. 3rd ed.
Eichinger, Ulrike (2009): Zwischen Anpassung und Ausstieg. Wiesbaden: VS.
Emmenegger, Patrick/Häusermann, Silja/Palier, Bruno/Seeleib-Kaiser, Martin (eds.) (2012): The age of dualization. The changing face of Inequlity in deindustrializing societies. Oxford: Oxford University Press.
Enggruber, Ruth/Fehlau, Michael (eds.) (2018): Jugendberufshilfe. Eine Einführung. Stuttgart: Kohlhammer Verlag.
Enggruber, Ruth/Fehlau, Michael (2021): Partizipation in einem arbeitsmarktpolitischen Angebot der Jugendberufshilfe aus Sicht der Teilnehmer_innen. In: Österreichisches Jahrbuch für Soziale Arbeit 3, 1, pp. 92–112.
Ennser-Jedenastik, Laurenz (2016): A Welfare State for Whom? A Group-based Account of the Austrian Freedom Party's Social Policy Profile. In: Swiss Political Science Review 22, 3, pp. 409–427.
Ennser-Jedenastik, Laurenz (2018a): Welfare Chauvinism in Populist Radical Right Platforms: The Role of Redistributive Justice Principles. In: Social Policy & Administration 52, 1, pp. 293–314.
Ennser-Jedenastik, Laurenz (2018b): Sozialpolitik ist die Achillesferse dieser Regierung. Ein Zurückfahren von Sozialleistungen würde die FPÖ wohl eher spüren als die ÖVP. In: Der Standard.
Esping-Andersen, Gøsta (1990): The three worlds of welfare capitalism. Princeton, N.J.: Princeton University Press.
Esping-Andersen, Gøsta (2002): A Child-Centered Social Investment Strategy. In: Esping-Andersen, Gøsta/Gallie, Duncan/Hemerijck, Anton/Myles, John (eds.): Why we need a new welfare state. New York: Oxford University Press, pp. 26–67.
Esping-Andersen, Gøsta (2003): Herkunft und Lebenschancen. Warum wir eine neue Politik gegen soziale Vererbung brauchen. In: Berliner Republik. Das Debattenmagazin.
Esping-Andersen, Gøsta (2008): Childhood investment and skill formation. In: International Tax and Public Finance 15, 1, pp. 19–44.
Esping-Andersen, Gøsta/Gallie, Duncan/Hemerijck, Anton/Myles, John (eds.) (2002): Why we need a new welfare state. New York: Oxford University Press.
European Commission (2015): The contribution of youth work to address the challenges young people are facing, in particular the transition from education to employment. Results of the expert group set up under the European Union Work Plan for Youth for 2014–2015. Brussels.
European Court of Justice (2018): Vorlage zur Vorabentscheidung – Richtlinie 2011/95/EU – Normen für den Inhalt des internationalen Schutzes – Flüchtlingseigenschaft – Art. 29 – Sozialhilfeleistungen – Unterschiedliche Behandlung – Flüchtlinge mit befristeter Aufenthaltsberechtigung.
European Parliament, European Council (2013): Directive 2013/33/EU of the European Parliament and of the Council of 26-06-2013 laying down standards for the reception of applicants for international protection. In: European Parliament/European Council (eds.): Official Journal of the European Union. Luxemburg.
Expert Council for Integration (Expertenrat für Integration) (2018): Integrationsbericht 2018. Wien.

Fabris, Verena/Knecht, Alban/Moser, Michaela/Rybaczek-Schwarz, Robert/Sallinger, Christine/Schenk, Martin (eds.) (2018): Achtung. Abwertung hat System. Vom Ringen um Anerkennung, Wertschätzung und Würde. Wien: VÖG.

Fairclough, Isabela/Fairclough, Norman (2012): Political discourse analysis. A method for advanced students. London: Routledge.

Fanon, Frantz (1982): Black skin, white mask. New York: Grove Press.

Fasching, Helga (2019): Unterstützungsmaßnahmen zur Ausbildungs- und Arbeitsmarktinklusion von behinderten und ausgrenzungsgefährdeten Jugendlichen in Österreich. In: Quenzel, Gudrun/Hurrelmann, Klaus (eds.): Handbuch Bildungsarmut. Wiesbaden: Springer VS, pp. 853–878.

Federal Chancellery (2013): Arbeitsprogramm der österreichischen Bundesregierung 2013-2018. Erfolgreich. Österreich. Wien.

Finis Siegler, Beate (2018): Ansätze zur Differenzierung des sozialwirtschaftlichen Geschehens nach Ebenen. In: Kohlhoff, Ludger/Grunwald, Klaus (eds.): Aktuelle Diskurse in der Sozialwirtschaft I. Perspektiven Sozialwirtschaft und Sozialmanagement. Wiesbaden: VS Springer, pp. 9–24.

Fink, Marcel/Leibetseder, Bettina (2019): Die österreichische Mindestsicherungsreform 2010: Von der Armuts- zur Arbeitsmarktpolitik. In: Österreichische Zeitschrift für Politikwissenschaft 48, 1, p. 19.

Fink, Marian/Rocha-Akis, Silvia (2018): Wirkung einer Einführung von Familienbonus und Kindermehrbetrag auf die Haushaltseinkommen. In: WIFO-Monatsberichte 91, 5, pp. 359–374.

Finkeldey, Lutz (2007): Verstehen. Soziologische Grundlagen zur Jugendberufshilfe. Wiesbaden: VS.

Fischer, Andrew M. (2020): The Dark Sides of Social Policy: From Neoliberalism to Resurgent Right-wing Populism. In: Development and Change 51, 2, pp. 371–397.

Fliedl, Rainer (2013): Probleme der Primärversorgung in der Kinder- und Jugendpsychiatrie. In: Pädiatrie & Pädologie (Österreich) 48, Supplement 1, pp. 85–90.

Fliedl, Rainer/Ecker, Berenike/Karwautz, A. (2020): Kinder- und jugendpsychiatrische Versorgung 2019 in Österreich – Stufen der Versorgung, Ist-Stand und Ausblick. In: Neuropsychiatrie. Klinik, Diagnostik, Therapie und Rehabilitation 34, 4, pp. 179–188.

Foa, Uriel G./Foa, Edna B. (1976): Resource theory of social exchange. In: Thibaut, John W./Spence, Janet T./Carson, Robert C./Brehm, Jack Williams (eds.): Contemporary topics in social psychology. Morristown, NJ: General Learning Press.

Forster, Edgar (2010): Kritik der Ökonomisierung. In: Widersprüche, 115.

Foucault, Michel (2004): Geschichte der Gouvernementalität II: Die Geburt der Biopolitik. Vorlesung am Collège de France 1978–1979. Suhrkamp Taschenbuch Wissenschaft, Vol. 1809. Frankfurt/M.: Suhrkamp.

FPÖ Bildungsinstitut (n.y. [2011]): Handbuch freiheitlicher Politik. Wien. 3rd ed.

Freier, Carolin (2015): Soziale Aktivierung von Arbeitslosen? Dissertation. Gesellschaft der Unterschiede, Vol. 38. Bielefeld: transcript.

Freller, Katharina (2022): Bedeutung und Beachtung des Kindeswohls in Österreich am Beispiel der Umsetzung im Asylverfahren. Diplomarbeit. Graz: Universität Graz.

Fuchs, Martin/Karwautz, Andreas (2017): Epidemiologie psychischer Störungen bei Kindern und Jugendlichen: Eine narrative Übersichtsarbeit unter Berücksichtigung österreichischer Daten. In: Neuropsychiatrie. Klinik, Diagnostik, Therapie und Re-

habilitation. Organ der Gesellschaft Österreichischer Nervenärzte und Psychiater 31, 3, pp. 96–102.
Gaupp, Nora (2013): Entstehungsbedingungen von Übergängen von der Schule in den Beruf aus qualitativer und quantitativer Perspektive. In: Forum Qualitative Sozialforschung/Forum: Qualitative Social Research, 2.
Gehrmann, Gerd/Müller, Klaus D. (eds.) (2010): Aktivierende Soziale Arbeit mit nichtmotivierten Klienten. Regensburg: Walhalla. 3rd ed.
Geisberger, Tamara (2021): Entwicklung und Verteilung der Niedriglohnbeschäftigung in Österreich und in der EU. In: Statistische Nachrichten, 9/2021, pp. 680–698.
Geisberger, Tamara/Knittler, Käthe (2010): Niedriglöhne und atypische Beschäftigung in Österreich. In: Statistische Nachrichten, 6, pp. 448–461.
Geiser, Kaspar (2015): Problem- und Ressourcenanalyse in der Sozialen Arbeit. Freiburg/Br.: Lambertus. 3rd ed.
Germain, Carel B./Gitterman, Alex (2021): The Life Model of Social Work Practice: Advances in Theory and Practice. New York: Columbia University Press. 2nd ed.
Gesslbauer, Ernst/Putz, Sabine/Sturm, René/Steiner, Karin (eds.): Herausforderungen an der Schnittstelle Schule – Beruf. Beiträge zur Fachtagung "Wege ebnen an der Schnittstelle Schule – Beruf. Wie gelingt ein erfolgreicher Übergang?" 18-09-2013 in Vienna. AMS report, Vol. 103. Wien.
Giddens, Anthony (1995): The Constitution of Society: Outline of the Theory of Structuration. Berkley: University of California Press.
Giddens, Anthony (2000): The Third Way: The Renewal of Social Democracy. Cambridge et al.: Polity Press.
Giesel, Katharina D. (2007): Leitbilder in den Sozialwissenschaften. Begriffe, Theorien und Forschungskonzepte. Wiesbaden: VS.
Glemser, Rolf/Gahleitner, Silke Brigitta (2012): Ressourcenorientierte Diagnostik. In: Knecht, Alban/Schubert, Franz-Christian (eds.): Ressourcen im Sozialstaat und in der Sozialen Arbeit. Zuteilung – Förderung – Aktivierung. Stuttgart: Kohlhammer, pp. 278–291.
Goffman, Erving (1952): On Cooling the Mark Out. In: Psychiatry 15, 4, pp. 451–463.
Gonon, Philipp (2002): Der Betrieb als Erzieher – Knappheit als pädagogische Herausforderung. In: Zeitschrift für Pädagogik 48, 3, pp. 317–335.
Götsch, Monika/Kessl, Fabian (2017): Editorial: Leben im transformierten Sozialstaat: Forschungsperspektiven aus der Sozialpolitik und der Sozialen Arbeit. In: Sozialer Fortschritt 66, ¾, pp. 179–194.
Graber, Renate/Widmann, Aloysius (2021): Neuer Erlass: Arbeitsmarkt soll für Asylwerber möglichst verschlossen bleiben. In: Der Standard.
Gray, Anne (2004): Unsocial Europe: Social Protection or Flexploitation. London: Pluto Press.
Gruber, Elke (2008): Berufsbildung in Österreich – Einblicke in einen bedeutenden Bildungssektor. In: Neß, Harry/Kimmig, Thomas (eds.): Kompendium zu aktuellen Herausforderungen beruflicher Bildung in Deutschland, Polen und Österreich. Frankfurt/M.: Deutsches Institut für Internationale Pädagogische Forschung, pp. 40–57.
Gučanin, Jelena (2013): "Schule kann ich mir nicht leisten". In: Der Standard, 09-04-2013. https://www.derstandard.at/story/1363707381400/schule-kann-ich-mir-nicht-leisten [access: 08-10-2023]

Hagen, Laura (2018): AMS-Kürzungen – Armutszeugnis und Zukunftsraub. Die von der Regierung geplante Kürzung beim Arbeitsmarktservice sorgt für Kritik. In: Standard.

Haider, Jörg (1994): Die Freiheit, die ich meine, Vol. 36629. Frankfurt/M., Berlin: Ullstein. 4th ed.

Haidinger, Bettina/Kaspar, Ruth/Knecht, Alban/Kuchler, Karin/Atzmüller, Roland (2016): Youth Policies and Gender-sensitive Youth Work in Austria. Evidence from a Capability-Oriented Perspective. A Compilation of National Case Study Reports from the EU-Project SocIEtY. FORBA Research Report. Wien.

Haidinger, Bettina/Knecht, Alban (2015): Chapter 18: Interventions of Gender-specific Youth Work in Vienna, Austria: Between Integration and Critique. In: SocIEtY Consortium (ed.): Collected Volume. Deliverable 3.3 des Projekts 'SocIEtY: Empowering the Young for the Common Good'. Bielefeld.

Hajer, Maarten A. (2008): Diskursanalyse in der Praxis: Koalitionen, Praktiken und Bedeutung. In: Janning, Frank/Toens, Katrin (eds.): Die Zukunft der Policy-Forschung. Theorien, Methoden, Anwendungen. Wiesbaden: VS, pp. 211–222.

Hall, Stuart (1986): Popular-demokratischer und autoritärer Populismus. In: Dubiel, Helmut (ed.): Populismus und Aufklärung. Frankfurt/M.: Suhrkamp, pp. 84–105.

Hall, Stuart (1996): The After-life of Frantz Fanon: Why Fanon? Why now? Why Black Skin, White Mask? In: Read, Alan (ed.): The fact of blackness. Frantz Fanon and visual representation. London: Institute of Contemporary Arts, pp. 12–37.

Hammer, Philipp (2018): Arbeitsmarktpolitik & Sozialstaat vor dem Umbau: Sind Existenzdruck & Sanktionen die Lösung? In: soziales kapital 20, pp. 166–179.

Hammerschmidt, Peter (2014): Zur Ökonomisierung der Sozialen Arbeit. In: Aulenbacher, Brigitte/Riegraf, Birgit/Theobald, Hildegard (eds.): Sorge: Arbeit, Verhältnisse, Regime. Soziale Welt, Sonderheft. Baden-Baden: Nomos, pp. 325–342.

Hanesch, Walter (2012): Ressourcenorientierung in der Armutsforschung – Perspektiven zu Familien- und Kinderarmut. In: Knecht, Alban/Schubert, Franz-Christian (eds.): Ressourcen im Sozialstaat und in der Sozialen Arbeit. Zuteilung – Förderung – Aktivierung. Stuttgart: Kohlhammer, pp. 146–156.

Hartwig, Luise (ed.) (2000): Parteilichkeit in der sozialen Arbeit. Forschung, Studium und Praxis, Vol. 4. Münster: Waxmann.

Heimgartner, Arno (2009): Komponenten einer prospektiven Entwicklung der Sozialen Arbeit. Wien: LIT.

Hellein, Bettina/Sturm, Florian/Hochreiter, Claudia (2014): Jugendrat – Quo vadis? Reflexionen aus drei Jugendräten in OÖ. Freistadt.

Hemerijck, Anton (2013): Changing Welfare States. Oxford: Oxford University Press.

Herriger, Norbert (2014): Empowerment in der Sozialen Arbeit. Eine Einführung. Stuttgart: Kohlhammer, 5th ed.

Herwartz-Emden, Leonie/Schurt, Verena/Waburg, Wiebke/Ruhland, Mandy (2008): Interkulturelle und geschlechtergerechte Pädagogik für Kinder im Alter von 6 bis 16 Jahren. Expertise für die Enquêtekommission des Landtages von Nordrhein-Westfalen "Chancen für Kinder".

Hesse, Friedrich W./Matt, Ina/Reckling, Falk/Völker, Thomas/Possanner, Nikolaus (2019): Standortbestimmung der Bildungsforschung in Österreich. Wien.

Hobfoll, Stevan E. (1988): The ecology of stress. Washington, DC: Hemisphere.

Hobfoll, Stevan E. (1989): Conservation of Resources – A New Attempt at Conceptualizing Stress. In: American Psychologist 44, 3, pp. 513–524.

Hobfoll, Stevan E./Jackson, A. P. (1991): Conservation of resources in Community Intervention. In: American Journal of Community Psychology 19, 1, pp. 111–121.
Hofbauer, Silvia/Kugi-Mazza, Edith/Sinowatz, Lisa (2014): Erfolgsmodell ÜBA: Eine Analyse der Effekte von Investitionen in die überbetriebliche Ausbildung (ÜBA) auf Arbeitsmarkt und öffentliche Haushalte. In: WISO 37, 3, pp. 50–66.
Hoff, Ernst/Lappe, Lothar/Lempert, Wolfgang (1982): Sozialisationstheoretische Überlegungen zur Analyse von Arbeit, Betrieb und Beruf. In: Soziale Welt 33, ¾, pp. 508–536.
Honneth, Axel (1992): Kampf um Anerkennung. Zur moralischen Grammatik sozialer Konflikte. Frankfurt/M.: Suhrkamp.
Horvath, Kenneth (2014): Die Logik der Entrechtung. Migrations- und Integrationsforschung. Göttingen: V&R unipress/Vienna University Press.
Hosner, Roland/Vana, Irina/Khun Jush, Golschan (2017): Integrationsmaßnahmen und Arbeitsmarkterfolg von Flüchtlingen und subsidiär Schutzberechtigen in Österreich. Forschungsprojekt des FIMAS Projekts. Wien.
IDB (2016–2019): Diskriminierung im österreichischen Bildungswesen. Berichte 2016–2019. Wien.
Jessop, Bob (2018): Neoliberalism and Workfare: Schumpeterian or Ricardian? In: Cahill, Damien/Cooper, Melinda/Konings, Martijn/Primrose, David (eds.): The SAGE Handbook of Neoliberalism. Los Angeles u. a.: SAGE, pp. 347–358.
John, Gerald (2017): Was an Kurz' These von der "Zuwanderung in den Sozialstaat" dran ist. In: Der Standard Wien, 16-07-2017. https://www.derstandard.at/story/2000061317804/was-an-kurz-these-von-der-zuwanderung-in-den-sozialstaat [access: 10-10-2023]
John, Gerald (2018): Regierung bestreitet trotz Sparplänen, dass Deutschkurse wegfallen. In: Der Standard, 16-07-2017. https://www.derstandard.at/story/2000061317804/was-an-kurz-these-von-der-zuwanderung-in-den-sozialstaat [access: 80-10-2023]
Jorck, Gerrit von/Gerold, Stefanie/Geiger, Sonja/Schrader, Ulf (2019): Arbeitspapier zur Definition von Zeitwohlstand im Forschungsprojekt ReZeitKon.
Jørgensen, Martin Bak/Thomsen, Trine Lund (2016): Deservingness in the Danish context: Welfare chauvinism in times of crisis. In: Critical Social Policy 36, 3, pp. 330–351.
Juhasz, Anne/Mey, Eva (2003): Die Zweite Generation. Biographien von Jugendlichen ausländischer Herkunft. Wiesbaden: VS.
Kähler, Harro Dietrich/Zobrist, Patrick (2013): Soziale Arbeit in Zwangskontexten. Wie unerwünscht Hilfe erfolgreich sein kann. München, Basel: Ernst Reinhardt. 2nd ed.
Kapeller, Doris/Stiftinger, Anna (2014): Bildungswünsche und -bedarfe von Frauen der Zweiten Generation. Standpunkt Bildung.
Karl, Ute/Schröder, Christian (2021): Ein- und Ausschließungsprozesse am und unter dem Existenzminimum: Junge Menschen im Hartz IV-Bezug. In: Anhorn, Roland/Stehr, Johannes (eds.): Handbuch Soziale Ausschließung und Soziale Arbeit. Springer eBook Collection, Vol. 26. Wiesbaden: Springer VS, pp. 969–986.
Kaufmann, Franz-Xaver (1973): Zum Verhältnis von Sozialarbeit und Sozialpolitik. In: Otto, Hans-Uwe/Schneider, Siegfried (eds.): Gesellschaftliche Perspektiven der Sozialarbeit. Erster Halbband. Neuwied, Berlin: Luchterhand, pp. 87–104.

Kaufmann, Franz-Xaver (2005): Sozialpolitik und Sozialstaat: Soziologische Analysen. Wiesbaden: VS. 2nd ed.
Keller, Reiner (2004): Diskursforschung. Eine Einführung für SozialwissenschaftlerInnen. Qualitative Sozialforschung. Wiesbaden: VS. 2nd ed.
Keller, Reiner (2006): Wissenssoziologische Diskursanalyse. In: Keller, Reiner/Hirseland, Andreas/Schneider, Werner/Viehöver, Willy (eds.): Handbuch sozialwissenschaftliche Diskursanalyse. Band 1: Theorien und Methoden. Wiesbaden: VS. 2nd ed., S. 115–146.
Kerle, Anja (2021): Das positiv-blickende Selbst als Schauplatz der Armutsbearbeitung. In: Sozial Extra 45, 3, S. 192–195.
Keskinen, Suvi (2016): From welfare nationalism to welfare chauvinism: Economic rhetoric, the welfare state and changing asylum policies in Finland. In: Critical Social Policy 36, 3, S. 352–370.
Kessl, Fabian (2013): Soziale Arbeit in der Transformation des Sozialen. Transformation des Sozialen – Transformation Sozialer Arbeit. Wiesbaden: Springer VS.
Kessl, Fabian (2018): Ökonomisierung. In: Böllert, Karin (ed.): Kompendium Kinder- und Jugendhilfe. Wiesbaden: Springer VS, S. 1629–1643.
Kessl, Fabian/Otto, Hans-Uwe (2002): Aktivierende Soziale Arbeit – Anmerkungen zu neosozialen Programmierungen Sozialer Arbeit. In: Neue Praxis, 5, S. 444–457.
Kessl, Fabian/Otto, Hans-Uwe (2003): Aktivierende Soziale Arbeit. Anmerkungen zur neosozialen Programmierung Sozialer Arbeit. In: Dahme, Heinz-Juergen/Otto, Hans-Uwe/Trube, Achim/Wohlfahrt, Norbert (eds.): Soziale Arbeit für den aktivierenden Staat. Wiesbaden: Leske + Budrich, S. 57–73.
Kessl, Fabian/Otto, Hans-Uwe (eds.) (2009): Soziale Arbeit ohne Wohlfahrtsstaat? Zeitdiagnosen, Problematisierungen und Perspektiven. Edition soziale Arbeit. Weinheim: Juventa.
Kessl, Fabian/Reutlinger, Christian/Ziegler, Holger (eds.) (2007): Erziehung zur Armut? Soziale Arbeit und die 'neue Unterschicht'. Wiesbaden: VS.
Kienbacher, Christian (2017): Seelische Gesundheit. In: Bericht zur Lage der Kinder- und Jugendgesundheit in Österreich 2017. Wien, S. 43–44.
Kienbacher, Christian (2018): Psychische Gesundheit im Kindes- und Jugendalter. In: Bericht zur Lage der Kinder- und Jugendgesundheit in Österreich 2018. Wien, S. 49–54.
Kindeswohl-Kommission (2021): Bericht der unabhängigen Kommission für den Schutz der Kindnerrechte und des Kindeswohls im Asyl- und Fremdenrecht. Wien.
Klammer, Uta (2012): Rush Hours of Life – Die Ressource Zeit im Lebenslauf aus Gender- und Familienperspektive. In: Knecht, Alban/Schubert, Franz-Christian (eds.): Ressourcen im Sozialstaat und in der Sozialen Arbeit. Zuteilung – Förderung – Aktivierung. Stuttgart: Kohlhammer, S. 117–131.
Klevenow, Gert-Holger/Knecht, Alban (2013): Soziale Diagnose in der Arbeitsverwaltung. In: Soziale Arbeit 62, 1, S. 18–24.
Knecht, Alban (2010): Lebensqualität produzieren. Ressourcentheorie und Machtanalyse des Wohlfahrtsstaats. Wiesbaden: VS.
Knecht, Alban (2011): Befähigungsstaat und Frühförderstaat als Leitbilder des 21. Jahrhunderts. Sozialpolitik mittels der Ressourcentheorie analysieren und gestalten. In: Wirtschaft und Gesellschaft 37, 4, S. 589–611.
Knecht, Alban (2012a): Ressourcentheoretische Erweiterungen des Capabilty-Ansatzes von Amartya Sen. In: Knecht, Alban/Schubert, Franz-Christian (eds.): Ressourcen

im Sozialstaat und in der Sozialen Arbeit. Zuteilung – Förderung – Aktivierung. Stuttgart: Kohlhammer, S. 61–71.

Knecht, Alban (2012b): Ressourcenzuteilung im Wohlfahrtsstaat – Sozialpolitische Perspektiven. In: Knecht, Alban/Schubert, Franz-Christian (eds.): Ressourcen im Sozialstaat und in der Sozialen Arbeit. Zuteilung – Förderung – Aktivierung. Stuttgart: Kohlhammer, S. 75–88.

Knecht, Alban (2012c): Understanding and Fighting Poverty – Amartya Sen's Capability Approach and Related Theories. In: Social Change Review 10, 2, S. 153–176.

Knecht, Alban (2014): Soziale Arbeit mit benachteiligten Jugendlichen in Zeiten der Krise: Emanzipatorische Befähigung versus Arbeitsmarktintegration. In: Soziale Passagen 6, 2, S. 219–236.

Knecht, Alban (2016): Die Bedeutung von psychischen Ressourcen für benachteiligte Jugendliche am Übergang von der Schule in Ausbildung und Beruf. In: Verhaltenstherapie & psychosoziale Praxis 48, 4. http://www.albanknecht.de/publikationen/Psychische-Ressourcen-benachteiligte-Jugendliche.pdf [access: 08-10-2023]

Knecht, Alban (2018): Sozialmissbrauch als Aufhänger. In: Augustin, 457, S. 12.

Knecht, Alban/Atzmüller, Roland (2017): Von der Ausbildungsgarantie zur Ausbildungspflicht. Die Entwicklung der österreichischen Beschäftigungspolitik für Jugendliche. In: Neue Praxis 47, 3, S. 239–252.

Knecht, Alban/Atzmüller, Roland (2019): Erschwertes Erwachsenwerden in der Berufsausbildung – Entwicklungen des Jugendregimes in Österreich. In: Heinen, Andreas/Wiezorek, Christine/Willems, Helmut (eds.): Entgrenzung der Jugend und Verjugendlichung der Gesellschaft – Zur Notwendigkeit einer 'Neuvermessung' jugendtheoretischer Konzeptionen. Weinheim, München: Beltz Juventa, S. 216–232.

Knecht, Alban/Atzmüller, Roland (2021): Lumping Asylum Seekers, Migration and the Poor together – Media Discourses and Welfare-Policy Dispositives in Austria After 2015. Presentation on the Conference "Summer of Migration" – Right-Wing Populism, Media and Affects, 16/17-09-2021, Ljubljana.

Knecht, Alban/Bodenstein, Michael (2019): Beschäftigungsförderung Jugendlicher unter der ÖVP-FPÖ-Regierung. Die österreichische Jugendberufshilfe zwischen wirtschaftskonservativer Arbeitsmarktintegration und rechtspopulistischer Diskriminierung. In: Sozial Extra 43, 3, S. 217–220.

Knecht, Alban/Buttner, Peter (2008): Die Ressourcentheorie in der Sozialen Arbeit. Armut besser verstehen. In: Standpunkt Sozial 1+2, S. 45–49.

Knecht, Alban/Kuchler, Karin/Atzmüller, Roland (2014): Youth Poverty, Youth Inequality, and Youth Policy in Austria. Experts' Perception of Youth Poverty and Inequality – Active Labour Market Policies and Youth Work – Opportunities of Participation – Social Innovation (chapter 15). In: SocIEtY Consortium (ed.): Youth Policies in European Countries and their Potential for Social Innovation. Deliverable 3.2 des Projekts 'SocIEtY: Empowering the Young for the Common Good'. Bielefeld, S. 494–541.

Knecht, Alban/Preite, Luca (2022): Politische Rahmenbedingungen der Beschäftigungsförderung benachteiligter Jugendlicher in Österreich und der Schweiz. In: Österreichisches Jahrbuch für Soziale Arbeit, 3, S. 125–143.

Knecht, Alban/Schenk, Martin (2023): Armutsforschung in Österreich zwischen Theorie und Empirie – aktuelle Entwicklungen. In: Sektion Soziale Ungleichheit/ Hof-

mann, Julia/Dlabaja, Cornelia (eds.): Handbuch soziale Ungleichheit. Weinheim u.a.: Juventa.
Knecht, Alban/Schubert, Franz-Christian (eds.) (2012): Ressourcen im Sozialstaat und in der Sozialen Arbeit. Zuteilung – Förderung – Aktivierung. Stuttgart: Kohlhammer.
Knecht, Alban/Schubert, Franz-Christian (2020): Konzeptualisierung einer transdisziplinären Ressourcentheorie für die Soziale Arbeit. In: Neue Praxis 50, 4, S. 310–320.
Knecht, Alban/Schubert, Franz-Christian/Gahleitner, Silke/Glemser, Rolf/Klevenow, Gert-Holger/Röh, Dieter (2014): Mit Ressourcenansätzen soziale Welten verstehen und Veränderungen aktivieren. In: Köttig, Michaela/Borrmann, Stefan/Effinger, Herbert et al. (eds.): Wahrnehmen, analysieren, intervenieren. Zugänge zu sozialen Wirklichkeiten in der Sozialen Arbeit. Theorie, Forschung und Praxis der Sozialen Arbeit, Vol. 9. Opladen: Barbara Budrich, S. 107–117.
Knecht, Alban/Tamesberger, Dennis (2019): Die türkis-blaue Arbeitsmarktpolitik für Jugendliche war widersprüchlich und ineffizient. https://awblog.at/tuerkis-blaue-arbeitsmarktpolitik-fuer-jugendliche [access: 22-10-2019].
Kohlrausch, Bettina (2014): Das Verhältnis von Bildungs- und Sozialpolitik im investiven Sozialstaat. In: Bauer, Ullrich/Bolder, Axel/Bremer, Helmut/Dobischat, Rolf/Kutscha, Günter (eds.): Expansive Bildungspolitik – Expansive Bildung? Bildung und Arbeit. Wiesbaden: Springer VS, S. 89–105.
Koning, Edward A. (2019): Immigration and the Politics of Welfare Exclusion. Selective solidarity in Western democracies. Studies in Comparative Political Economy and Public Policy, Vol. 55. Toronto, Buffalo, London: University of Toronto Press, Scholarly Publishing Division.
Kourabas, Veronika/Mecheril, Paul (2022): Über Rassismus sprechen. Auf dem Weg zu einer rassismuskritischen Professionalität. In: Stock, Miriam/Hodaie, Nazli/Immerfall, Stefan/Menz, Margarete (eds.): Arbeitstitel: Migrationsgesellschaft. Pädagogik – Profession – Praktik. MiGS: Migration – Gesellschaft – Schule. Wiesbaden: Springer VS, S. 13–33.
Kraus, Katrin (2007): Vom Beruf zur Employability? Zur Theorie einer Pädagogik des Erwerbs. Wiesbaden: VS.
Kreckel, Reinhard (2004): Politische Soziologie der sozialen Ungleichheit. Theorie und Gesellschaft, Vol. 25. Frankfurt/New York: Campus. 3rd ed.
Krisch, Richard (2011): Bildung und Ausbildung im Kontext von Jugendarbeit. In: BMWFJ (ed.): 6. Bericht zur Lage der Jugend in Österreich. Wien, pp. 503–516.
Kuklys, Wiebke (2005): Amartya Sen's Capability Approach. Theoretical Insights and Empirical Applications. Berlin, Heidelberg: Springer.
Kurier (2016a): Regierung beschließt "Asyl auf Zeit". In: Kurier, 26-01-2016. Wien.
Kurier (2016b): Hofer will "Invasion der Muslime" stoppen. In: Kurier 02-04-2016. Wien
Lachmayr, Norbert/Mayerl, Martin (2019): 3. Österreichischer Lehrlingsmonitor. Ergebnisse einer bundesweiten Befragung von Lehrlingen im letzten Lehrjahr. Endbericht. Wien.
Laclau, Ernesto/Mouffe, Chantal (1991): Hegemonie und radikale Demokratie. Zur Dekonstruktion des Marxismus. Wien: Passagen.
Langthaler, Herbert (2019): Lehrlinge und kein Ende. In: Asyl Aktuell, 3, pp. 2–7.

Laruffa, Francesco (2018): Towards a Post-Liberal Social Policy? Social Investment versus Capability Approach. In: Momentum Quarterly 7, 4, pp. 171–187.
Lassnigg, Lorenz (1999): Youth Labour Market Policy in Austria. Sociological Studies, 38. Wien. http://www.equi.at/dateien/rs38.pdf [access: 08-12-2022].
Lassnigg, Lorenz (2016): "Duale" oder "dualistische" Berufsausbildung: Gemeinsamkeiten und Unterschiede Österreich-Schweiz-Deutschland. In: Seifried, Jürgen/Seeber, Susan/Ziegler, Birgit (eds.): Jahrbuch der berufs- und wirtschaftspädagogischen Forschung. Schriftenreihe der Sektion Berufs- und Wirtschaftspädagogik der Deutschen Gesellschaft für Erziehungswissenschaften. Opladen, Berlin, Toronto: Barbara Budrich.
Lazarus, Richard/Folkman, Susan (1984): Stress, Appraisal, and Coping. New York: Springer.
Lefkofridi, Zoe/Michel, Elie (2017): The electoral politics of solidarity the welfare agendas of radical right parties. In: Banting, Keith G./Kymlicka, Will (eds.): The strains of commitment: The political sources of solidarity in diverse societies. Oxford: Oxford University Press, S. 233–267.
Lehmkuhl, Kirsten/Schmidt, Guido/Schöler, Cornelia (2013): "Ihr seid nicht dumm, ihr seid nur faul." – Über die wunderliche Leistung, Ausgrenzung als selbstverschuldet erleben zu lassen. In: Maier, Maja S./Vogel, Thomas (eds.): Übergänge in eine neue Arbeitswelt? Blinde Flecken der Debatte zum Übergangssystem Schule-Beruf. Wiesbaden: Springer VS.
Lehner, Sabine/Wodak, Ruth (2020): Nationalismus und Rechtspopulismus. In: Cillia, Rudolf de/Wodak, Ruth/Rheindorf, Markus/Lehner, Sabine (eds.): Österreichische Identitäten im Wandel: Empirische Untersuchungen zu ihrer diskursiven Konstruktion 1995–2015. Wiesbaden: Springer VS, S. 169–204.
Lehnert, Katrin (2009): "Arbeit, nein danke"!? Das Bild des Sozialschmarotzers im aktivierenden Sozialstaat. Münchner ethnographische Schriften. München: Herbert Utz.
Leibetseder, Bettina (2016): Die Sozialinvestitionsperspektive der Europäischen Union – ein neoliberaler Wolf im Schafspelz? In: SWS-Rundschau 55, 1, pp. 48–66.
Lendvai-Bainton, Noemi/Szelewa, Dorota (2020): Governing new authoritarianism: Populism, nationalism and radical welfare reforms in Hungary and Poland. In: Social Policy & Administration 55, 4, pp. 559–572.
Lessenich, Stephan (2004): Ökonomismus zum Wohlfühlen: Gøsta Esping-Andersen und die neue Architektur des Sozialstaats. In: PROKLA. Zeitschrift für kritische Sozialwissenschaft 34, 136 [3], pp. 469–476.
Lessenich, Stephan (2008): Die Neuerfindung des Sozialen. X-Texte zu Kultur und Gesellschaft. Bielefeld: transcript.
Lessenich, Stephan (2009): Mobilität und Kontrolle. Zur Dialektik der Aktivgesellschaft. In: Dörre, Klaus/Lessenich, Stephan/Rosa, Hartmut (eds.): Soziologie – Kapitalismus – Kritik. Eine Debatte. Frankfurt/M.: Suhrkamp, pp. 126–177.
Lessenich, Stephan (2012): Constructing the socialized self. Mobilization and control in the "active society". In: Bröckling, Ulrich/Krasmann, Susanne/Lemke, Thomas (eds.): Governmentality. Current issue and future challenge. New York, London: Routledge, pp. 304–319.
Leßmann, Ortrud/Otto, Hans-Uwe/Ziegler, Holger (eds.) (2011): Closing the Capability Gap. Negotiating social justice for the young. Opladen, Farmington Hills, MI: Barbara Budrich.

Lindberg, Annika (2020): The production of Precarity in Denmark's Asylum Regime. In: Zeitschrift für Sozialreform/Journal for Social Policy Research 66, 4, pp. 413–439.
Link, Jürgen (2007): Dispositiv und Interdiskurs. Mit Überlegungen zum Dreieck Foucault – Bourdieu – Luhmann. In: Kammler, Clemens/Parr, Rolf (eds.): Foucault in den Kulturwissenschaften. Eine Bestandsaufnahme. Heidelberg: Synchron Wiss. – Verlag der Autoren, pp. 219–238.
Lipksy, Michael (1980): Street-level bureaucracy. Dilemmas of the individual in public sevices. New York: Russel Sage Foundation.
Löffler, Marion (2018): Alles Retro? Die neu-konservative Wende in Österreich. In: Femina Politica. Zeitschrift für feministische Politikwissenschaft 27, 1, pp. 121–127.
Ludwig-Mayerhofer, Wolfgang/Behrend, Olaf/Sondermann, Ariadne (2009): Auf der Suche nach der verlorenen Arbeit. Arbeitslose und Arbeitsvermittler im neuen Arbeitsmarktregime. Analyse und Forschung Sozialwissenschaften. Konstanz: UVK.
Lutz, Tilman (2010): Soziale Arbeit im Kontrolldiskurs. Jugendhilfe und ihre Akteure in postwohlfahrtsstaatlichen Gesellschaften. Perspektiven kritischer Sozialer Arbeit, Vol. 9. Wiesbaden: VS.
Lutz, Tilman (2013): Kontrollorientierung der Sozialen Arbeit im aktivierenden Staat. In: Sozial Extra, 9/10, pp. 25–28.
Maier, Maja S. (2013): 'Schule ist Schrott' – Jugendliche Selbstbehauptung und pädagogische Praktiken im Spannungsfeld von Aktivierungspolitik und der Pädagogik am Übergang. In: Maier, Maja S./Vogel, Thomas (eds.): Übergänge in eine neue Arbeitswelt? Blinde Flecken der Debatte zum Übergangssystem Schule-Beruf. Wiesbaden: Springer VS, pp. 203–223.
Mairhuber, Ingrid/Atzmüller, Roland (2009): Zeitpolitik in Wien – Politik zur Sicherung der Lebensqualität. FORBA-Forschungsbericht 1/2009.
Marbach, Moritz/Hainmueller, Jens/Hangartner, Dominik (2018): The long-term impact of employment bans on the economic integration of refugees. In: Science advances 4, 9.
Marshall, Thomas Humphrey/Bottomore, Thomas B. (1992): Citizenship and social class. London: Pluto Press.
Mayrhofer, Monika (2006): »Was Männer bewegt« – Neokonservative Männlichkeitspolitik in Österreich im Kontext der Einrichtung der Männerpolitischen Grundsatzabteilung. In: Feministische Studien 24, 2, S. 276–289.
Melinz, Gerhard (1986): Jugendarbeitslosigkeit und ihre staatliche und sozialarbeiterische Bearbeitung in Österreich. In: Verein für Gesellschaftsgeschichte (ed.): Zwischen den Mühlsteinen von Arbeitsmarktpolitik und Kapital: Erwerbslosigkeit im 20. Jahrhundert. Wien: Verlag für Gesellschaftsgeschichte, pp. 68–90.
Metz, Marina (2016): Migration – Ressourcen – Biographie. Eine Studie über Zugewanderte aus der ehemaligen Sowjetunion. Beiträge zur Regional- und Migrationsforschung. Wiesbaden: Springer VS.
Meulemann, Heiner (2004): Sozialstruktur, soziale Ungleichheit und die Bewertung der ungleichen Verteilung von Ressourcen. In: Berger, Peter/Schmidt, Volker H. (eds.): Welche Gleichheit, welche Ungleichheit? Grundlagen der Ungleichheitsforschung. Wiesbaden: VS, pp. 115–136.
Möbius, Thomas/Friedrich, Sibylle (2010): Ressourcenorientiert Arbeiten. Anleitung zu einem gelingenden Praxistransfer im Sozialbereich. Wiesbaden: VS.

Morel, Nathalie/Palier, Bruno/Palme, Joakim (eds.) (2012): Towards a social investment welfare state? Ideas, policies and challenges. Bristol: Bristol University Press; Policy Press.

Muckenhuber, Johanna (2014): Arbeit ohne Ende? Zur Arbeitsrealität der "neuen" Selbstständigen. Konstanz, München: UVK.

Mudde, Cas/Rovira Kaltwasser, Cristóbal (2019): Populismus. Bonn: Dietz.

Müller, Hans-Peter (2015): Meritokratie als Schimäre. Gleichheit und Ungleichheit in Bildungsprozessen und die Folgen. In: Müller, Hans-Peter/Reitz, Tilman (eds.): Bildung und Klassenbildung. Kritische Perspektiven auf eine Leitinstitution der Gegenwart. Wirtschaft, Gesellschaft und Lebensführung. Weinheim: Beltz Juventa, pp. 104–122.

Münch, Sybille (2016): Interpretative Policy-Analyse. Eine Einführung. Wiesbaden: Springer VS.

Neumayr, Michaela (2012): Ressourcen der öffentlichen Hand: Finanzielle Abhängigkeit von Non-Profit-Organisationen und ihre Folgen. In: Knecht, Alban/Schubert, Franz-Christian (eds.): Ressourcen im Sozialstaat und in der Sozialen Arbeit. Zuteilung – Förderung – Aktivierung. Stuttgart: Kohlhammer, pp. 172–186.

Niedermair, Gerhard (ed.) (2017): Berufliche Benachteiligtenförderung. Theoretische Einsichten, empirische Befunde und aktuelle Maßnahmen. Schriftenreihe für Berufs- und Betriebspädagogik, Vol. 10. Linz: Trauner.

Nullmeier, Frank/Rüb, Friedbert (1993): Die Transformation der Sozialpolitik. Vom Sozialstaat zum Sicherungsstaat. Frankfurt, New York: Campus.

Nussbaum, Martha (1999): Gerechtigkeit oder das gute Leben. Frankfurt/M.: Suhrkamp.

Obinger, Herbert/Tálos, Emmerich (2006): Sozialstaat Österreich zwischen Kontinuität und Umbau. Eine Bilanz der ÖVP/FPÖ/BZÖ-Koalition. Wiesbaden: VS.

OECD (2019): OECD Reviews of Vocational Education and Training. Paris.

Oehme, Andreas/Beran, Christina M./Krisch, Richard (2007): Neue Wege in der Bildungs- und Beschäftigungsförderung für Jugendliche. Wissenschaftliche Reihe des VWJUZ, Vol. 4. Wien

öibf/IHS (2019): AusBildung bis 18. Wissenschaftliche Begleitung der Implementierung und Umsetzung des Ausbildungspflichtgesetzes. Wien.

Okkolin, Mari-Anne/Koskela, Teija/Engelbrecht, Petra/Savolainen, Hannu (2018): Capability to be Educated—Inspiring and Inclusive Pedagogical Arrangements from Finnish Schools. In: Journal of Human Development and Capabilities 19, 4, pp. 421–437.

Opielka, Michael (ed.) (2005a): Bildungsreform als Sozialreform. Zum Zusammenhang von Bildungs- und Sozialpolitik. Wiesbaden: VS.

Opielka, Michael (2005b): Wohlfahrt und Gerechtigkeit. Ideenanalyse in der Soziologie der Sozialpolitik. Besprechungsessay. In: Kölner Zeitschrift für Soziologie und Sozialpsychologie 57, 3, pp. 551–599.

ORF (2021): Diskriminierung meist ohne Konsequenzen. orf.at-Stories. Wien. https://oesterreich.orf.at/stories/3055585 [access: 26-12-2022].

Oschmiansky, Frank/Schmid, Günther/Kull, Silke (2003): Faule Arbeitslose? Politische Konjunkturen und Strukturprobleme der Missbrauchsdebatte. In: Leviathan 31, 1, pp. 3–31.

Ostheim, Tobias/Schmidt, Manfred G. (2007): Die Machtressourcentheorie. In: Schmidt, Manfred G. (ed.): Der Wohlfahrtsstaat. Eine Einführung in den historischen und internationalen Vergleich. Wiesbaden: VS, pp. 40–50.

Otto, Hans-Uwe/Egdell, Valerie/Bonvin, Jean-Michel/Atzmüller, Roland (eds.) (2017): Empowering Young People in Disempowering Times. Fighting Inequality Through Capability Oriented Policy. Cheltenham, UK/Northhampton, MA: Edward Elgar.

Otto, Hans-Uwe/Schrödter, Mark (2007): Befähigungsgerechtigkeit statt Bildungsgerechtigkeit. Zum Verhältnis von Gerechtigkeit und Effizienz. In: Grunert, Cathleen/Wensierski, Hans-Jürgen von (eds.): Jugend und Bildung. Modernisierungsprozesse und Strukturwandel von Erziehung und Bildung am Beginn des 21. Jahrhunderts. Opladen, Farmington Hills, Mich.: Budrich, pp. 55–77.

Otto, Hans-Uwe/Walker, Melanie/Ziegler, Holger (2018): Capability-Promoting Policies. Enhancing Individual and Social Development. Bristol: Bristol University Press, Policy Press.

Otto, Hans-Uwe/Ziegler, Holger (eds.) (2010a): Capabilities – Handlungsbefähigung und Verwirklichungschancen in der Erziehungswissenschaft. Wiesbaden: VS. 2nd ed.

Otto, Hans-Uwe/Ziegler, Holger (2010b): Der Capabilities-Ansatz als neue Orientierung in der Erziehungswissenschaft. In: Otto, Hans-Uwe/Ziegler, Holger (eds.): Capabilities – Handlungsbefähigung und Verwirklichungschancen in der Erziehungswissenschaft. Wiesbaden: VS. 2nd ed., pp. 9–13.

ÖVP/FPÖ (2017): Zusammen. Für unser Österreich. Regierungsprogramm 2017–2022. Wien.

Patrick, Ruth (2016): Living with and responding to the 'scrounger' narrative in the UK: exploring everyday strategies of acceptance, resistance and deflection. In: Journal of Poverty and Social Justice 24, 3, pp. 245–259.

Peck, Jamie (2001): Workfare States. New York, London: Guilford Press.

Pelizzari, Alessandro (2009): Dynamiken der Prekarisierung. Atypische Erwerbsverhältnisse und milieuspezifische Unsicherheitsbewältigung. Analyse und Forschung Sozialwissenschaften, Vol. 63. Konstanz: UVK.

Peternel, Evelyn/Bachner, Michael (2018): Arbeitslos in Österreich: Alles "Durchschummler" oder was? In: Kurier, 14-01-2018. https://kurier.at/politik/inland/arbeitslos-in-oesterreich-alles-durchschummler-oder-was/306.372.171 [access: 11-10-2023]

Philipp, Julia/Zeiler, Michael/Waldherr, Karin/Truttmann, Stefanie/Dür, Wolfgang/Karwautz, Andreas F. K./Wagner, Gudrun (2018): Prevalence of emotional and behavioral problems and subthreshold psychiatric disorders in Austrian adolescents and the need for prevention. In: Social Psychiatry and Psychiatric Epidemiology 53, 12, pp. 1325–1337.

Pichl, Maximilian (2017): Diskriminierung von Flüchtlingen und Geduldeten. In: Scherr, Albert/El-Mafaalani, Aladin/Yüksel, Gökçen (eds.): Handbuch Diskriminierung. Wiesbaden: Springer VS, pp. 449–463.

Plener, Paul L./Klier, Claudia M./Thun-Hohenstein, Leonhard/Sevecke, Kathrin (2021): Psychische Versorgung von Kindern und Jugendlichen in Österreich neu aufstellen: Dringender Handlungsbedarf besteht JETZT. In: Neuropsychiatrie 35, 4, pp. 213–215.

Pregel, Annedore (2013): Pädagogische Beziehungen zwischen Anerkennung, Verletzung und Ambivalenz. Opladen, Berlin, Toronto: Barbara Budrich.
Preite, Luca (2019): Jugendliche Handlungsfähigkeit wider die Praktiken des Cooling-Out: Eine Fallstudie am Beispiel von drei männlichen Jugendlichen im Schweizer Übergangsregime. In: Zeitschrift für Soziologie der Erziehung und Sozialisation 39, 4, pp. 384–399.
Preite, Luca (2021): Berufliche Grundbildung gegen Bezahlung. In: Widerspruch (Schweiz) 40, 76, pp. 41–47.
Preite, Luca (2022): Widerstand als Selbstbehauptung. »Gefährdete« Jugendliche im Übergangs- und Berufsbildungssystem. Gesellschaft der Unterschiede. Bielefeld: transcript.
Ptak, Ralf (2008): Grundlagen des Neoliberalismus. In: Butterwegge, Christoph/Lösch, Bettina/Ptak, Ralf (eds.): Kritik des Neoliberalismus. Wiesbaden: VS. 2nd ed., pp. 13–86.
Rawls, John (2005): A Theory of Justice. Cambridge, MA: Harvard University Press.
Reckinger, Gilles (2010): Perspektive Prekarität. Wege benachteiligter Jugendlicher in den transformierten Arbeitsmarkt. Konstanz: UVK.
Reckwitz, Andreas (2016): Praktiken und Diskurse. Zur Logik von Praxis-/Diskursformationen. In: Reckwitz, Andreas (ed.): Kreativität und soziale Praxis. Studien zur Sozial- und Gesellschaftstheorie. Bielefeld: transcript, pp. 49–66.
Reinders, Heinz (2016): Vom Bildungs- zum Optimierungsmoratorium. In: Diskurs Kinderheits- und Jugendforschung, 2, pp. 147–160.
Reinders, Heinz/Wild, Elke (eds.) (2003): Jugendzeit – Time Out? Zur Ausgestaltung des Jugendalters als Moratorium. Lehrtexte Soziologie. Opladen: Leske + Budrich.
Reisenzaun, Isabella (2016): "Halt die Pappn und hackl einfach!" Eine qualitative Untersuchung der Arbeits- und Ausbildungserfahrungen von Lehrlingen in der Gastronomie. Masterthesis. Wien: Universität.
Republic of Austria (1998): 91. Bundesgesetz: Jugendausbildungs-Sicherungsgesetz. In: Bundesgesetzblatt für die Republik Österreich 1998, Teil I, pp. 837–839.
Republic of Austria (2000): 83. Bundesgesetz: Änderung des Berufsausbildungsgesetzes und weiterer Gesetze. In: Bundesgesetzblatt für die Republik Österreich 2000, Teil I, pp. 809–811.
Republic of Austria (2003): 71. Bundesgesetz: Budgetbegleitgesetz 2003. In: Bundesgesetzblatt für die Republik Österreich 2003, Teil I, pp. 1041–1247.
Republic of Austria (2016): 62. Bundesgesetz: Jugendausbildungsgesetz (Ausbildungspflichtgesetz). In: Bundesgesetzblatt für die Republik Österreich, Teil I.
Republic of Austria (2018): 53. Bundesgesetz: Änderungen des Arbeitszeitgesetzes, des Arbeitsruhegesetzes und des Allgemeinen Sozialversicherungsgesetzes. In: Bundesgesetzblatt für die Republik Österreich 2018, Teil I.
Rieger, Günter (2016): Politologie/Politikwissenschaft und methodisches Handeln in der Sozialen Arbeit. In: Michel-Schwartze, Brigitta (ed.): Der Zugang zum Fall. Beobachtungen, Deutungen, Interventionsansätze. Wiesbaden: Springer VS, pp. 119–134.
Robeyns, Ingrid (2005): The Capability Approach: a theoretical survey. In: Journal of Human Development Vol. 6, 1, pp. 93–114.
Röh, Dieter (2012): Ressourcenorientierung in der Sozialen Arbeit – Einführung in Ressourcenorientierung in der Sozialen Arbeit – Einführung in Theorie und professionelle Methodik. In: Knecht, Alban/Schubert, Franz-Christian (eds.): Res-

sourcen im Sozialstaat und in der Sozialen Arbeit. Zuteilung – Förderung – Aktivierung. Stuttgart: Kohlhammer, pp. 189–204.
Röh, Dieter (2013): Soziale Arbeit, Gerechtigkeit und das gute Leben. Eine Handlungstheorie zur daseinsmächtigen Lebensführung. Soziale Arbeit in Theorie und Wissenschaft. Wiesbaden: Springer VS.
Rose, Nikolas (2000): Das Regieren von unternehmerischen Individuen. In: Kurswechsel, 2, pp. 8–27.
Rose, Stephanie (2018): Das Reproduktionsregime. Sicherung von Arbeits- und Lebenskraft zwischen Effizienz und Resilienz. Springer VS.
Rosenberger, Sieglinde/Schmid, Gabriele (2003): Treffsicher. Sozialpolitik zwischen 2000 und 2002. In: Rosenberger, Sieglinde/Tálos, Emmerich (eds.): Sozialstaat. Probleme, Herausforderungen, Perspektiven. Wien: mandelbaum, pp. 96–120.
Röth, Leonce/Afonso, Alexandre/Spies, Dennis C. (2018): The impact of Populist Radical Right Parties on socio-economics policies. In: European Political Science Review 10, 3, pp. 325–350.
Rothmüller, Barbara (2014): Bildungspolitische Theorieeffekte und ihre Komplizenschaft mit Ungleichheiten. In: Kastner, Jens/Sonderegger, Ruth (eds.): Pierre Bourdieu und Jacques Rancière. Emanzipatorische Praxis denken. Wien, Berlin: Verlag Turia + Kant, pp. 147–182.
Sabatella, Filomena/Wyl, Agnes von (eds.) (2018): Jugendliche im Übergang zwischen Schule und Beruf. Psychische Belastungen und Ressourcen. Berlin: Springer.
Sallmuter, Hans (2002): Halbzeit von »Österreich neu regieren«. Eine Bewertung und Bilanz aus dem Blickwinkel der Sozialversicherung. Blog Arbeit & Wirtschaft. Wien.
Salzburger Nachrichten (2017): Kurz begrüßt Kerns Plan für Bedarfsprüfung am Arbeitsmarkt. In: Salzburger Nachrichten.
Sandel, Michael J. (2012): What Money Can't Buy: The Moral Limits of Markets. New York: Farrar, Straus and Giroux.
Sanduvac, Seher (2018): Ökonomisierung der Sozialen Arbeit am Beispiel Jugendcoaching. Masterarbeit. Linz: Johannes-Kepler-Universität.
Sator, Andreas (2018): Die FPÖ profitiert von gescheiterter Integration. In: Die Zeit.
Schatz, Birgit et al. (2017): Entschließungsantrag betreffend der Ausbildungspflicht bis 18 Jahre für jugendliche AsylwerberInnen. Wien.
Schenk, Martin (2015): Unsoziale Übertreiber. In: Augustin (Wien), 399, p. 2
Scherschel, Karin/Streckeisen, Peter/Krenn, Manfred (eds.) (2012): Neue Prekarität. Die Folgen aktivierender Arbeitsmarktpolitik – Europäische Länder im Vergleich. Labour Studies, Vol. 2. Frankfurt/M., New York: Campus.
Schlögl, Peter (2016): AusBildung bis 18: Schonraum, Förderphase oder Zwang? In: Erziehung und Unterricht 166, 7–8, pp. 709–717.
Schlögl, Peter/Mayerl, Martin/Löffler, Roland/Schmölz, Alexander (2020): Supra-company apprenticeship training in Austria: a synopsis of empirical findings on a possibly early phase of a new pillar within VET. In: Empirical Research in Vocational Education and Training 12, 1, pp. 1–17.
Schmid, Gabriele (n.d.): Vier Jahre schwarz-blaue Sozialpolitik. Ein Schaustück in zwei Akten. In: Arbeit & Wirtschaft.
Schmidhofer, David (2013): Wie man zum Anarchisten gemacht wird: Zivildienst – moderne Zwangsarbeit in Österreich. Berlin: Autumnus.

Schmidt, Dorothea (2018): Gefahren beschwören, Risiken leugnen: rechte Parteien und Sozialstaat. In: Betzelt, Sigrid/Bode, Ingo (eds.): Angst im neuen Wohlfahrtsstaat. Kritische Blicke auf ein diffuses Phänomen. HWR Berlin Forschung, Vol. 64. Baden-Baden: Nomos, pp. 31–54.

Schneeberger, Arthur (2009): Bildungsgarantie bis zum 18./19. Lebensjahr. Entwicklungen und Perspektiven in der Berufsbildung. In: Specht, Werner (Hrsg.): Nationaler Bildungsbericht 2009, Bd. 2, Graz: Leykam. pp. 55–72.

Schönherr, Daniel/Leibetseder, Bettina/Moser, Winfried/Hofinger, Christoph (2019): Diskriminierungserfahrungen in Österreich. Erleben von Ungleichbehandlung, Benachteilung und Herabwürddigung in den Bereichen Arbeit, Wohnen, medizinische Dienstleistungen und Ausbildung. Endbericht. https://www.arbeiterkammer.at/interessenvertretung/arbeitundsoziales/gleichbehandlung/Diskriminierungsstudie_2019.pdf [access: 28-12-2022].

Schroeder, Gerhard/Blair, Tony (1999): Europe – The Third Way/Die neue Mitte ("The Schroeder-Blair-Paper") [A proposal by Gerhard Schröder and Tony Blair of 8 June 1999]. In: Blätter für deutsche und internationale Politik, 7, pp. 887–896.

Schubert, Franz-Christian (2012): Psychische Ressourcen – Zentrale Konstrukte in der Ressourcenkonstruktion. In: Knecht, Alban/Schubert, Franz-Christian (eds.): Ressourcen im Sozialstaat und in der Sozialen Arbeit. Zuteilung – Förderung – Aktivierung. Stuttgart: Kohlhammer, pp. 205–237.

Schubert, Franz-Christian (2013): Systemisch-sozialökologische Beratung. In: Nestmann, Frank/Engel, Frank/Sickendiek, Ursula (eds.): Neue Beratungswelten. Fortschritte und Kontroversen, Vol. 3. Tübingen: DGVT, pp. 1483–1505.

Schubert, Franz-Christian (2016): Ressourcenorientierung im Kontext von Lebensführung. Grundlegende Theorien und konzeptionelle Entwicklungen. In: Verhaltenstherapie & psychosoziale Praxis 48, pp. 827–844.

Schubert, Franz-Christian (2021a): Ressourcenaktivierung. In: Wälte, Dieter/Borg-Laufs, Michael (eds.): Psychosoziale Beratung. Grundlagen, Diagnostik, Intervention. Grundwissen Soziale Arbeit, Vol. 24. Stuttgart: Kohlhammer. 2nd ed., pp. 198–213.

Schubert, Franz-Christian (2021b): Ressourcendiagnostik. In: Wälte, Dieter/Borg-Laufs, Michael (eds.): Psychosoziale Beratung. Grundlagen, Diagnostik, Intervention. Grundwissen Soziale Arbeit, Vol. 24. Stuttgart: Kohlhammer. 2nd ed., pp. 117–134.

Schubert, Franz-Christian/Knecht, Alban (2012a): Einführung. In: Knecht, Alban/Schubert, Franz-Christian (eds.): Ressourcen im Sozialstaat und in der Sozialen Arbeit. Zuteilung – Förderung – Aktivierung. Stuttgart: Kohlhammer, pp. 9–12.

Schubert, Franz-Christian/Knecht, Alban (2012b): Ressourcen – Einführung in Merkmale, Theorien und Konzeptionen. In: Knecht, Alban/Schubert, Franz-Christian (eds.): Ressourcen im Sozialstaat und in der Sozialen Arbeit. Zuteilung – Förderung – Aktivierung. Stuttgart: Kohlhammer, pp. 15–41.

Schubert, Franz-Christian/Knecht, Alban (2015): Ressourcen – Merkmale, Theorien und Konzeptionen im Überblick. https://nbn-resolving.org/urn:nbn:de:0168-ssoar-50698-1.

Schubert, Franz-Christian/Knecht, Alban (2016): Vorwort der Herausgeber zum Schwerpunkt "Ressourcenperspektive öffnen!". In: Verhaltenstherapie & psychosoziale Praxis 48, 4, pp. 821–824.

Schubert, Franz-Christian/Knecht, Alban (2020): Resources – Features, Theories and Concepts at a Glance. Unpublished.
Schubert, Franz-Christian/Rohr, D./Zwicker-Pelzer, R. (2019): Beratung. Grundlagen – Konzepte – Anwendungsfelder. Heidelberg: Springer.
Schubert, Klaus/Bandelow, Nils C. (2014): Lehrbuch der Politikfeldanalyse. München: de Gruyter Oldenbourg. 3rd ed.
Schwarze, Uwe (2012): Sozialhilfe in Schweden und Deutschland. Wiesbaden: VS.
Sen, Amartya (1985): Commodities and Capabilities. Amsterdam, New York, Oxford: Elsevier Science Publishers.
Sen, Amartya (1990): Justice: Means versus Freedom. In: Philosophie & Public Affairs 19, 2, pp. 111–121.
Sen, Amartya (ed.) (1992): Inequality reexamined. Cambridge, Massachusetts: Harvard University Press.
Sen, Amartya (1999): Development as Freedom. New York: Alfred A. Knopf.
Simon, Stephanie/Lochner, Barbara/Prigge, Jessica (2019): Wie(so) über Armut sprechen? Zur Notwendigkeit einer armutsbewussten Praxis in Kindertagesstätten. In: Frühe Kindheit, 3, pp. 36–41.
SMS (2019): NEBA Jahresbericht 2019. Wien
SMS (2021): Jugendcoaching Umsetzungsregeln. Version vom 1.1.2021. Wien.
SocIEtY Consortium (ed.) (2014): Youth Policies in European Countries and their Potential for Social Innovation. Deliverable 3.2 des Projekts 'SocIEtY: Empowering the Young for the Common Good'. Bielefeld.
Solga, Heike (2008): Meritokratie – die moderne Legitimation ungleicher Bildungschancen. In: Berger, Peter A./Kahlert, Heike (eds.): Institutionalisierte Ungleichheiten. Wie das Bildungswesen Chancen blockiert. Bildungssoziologische Beiträge. Weinheim, München: Juventa. 2nd ed., pp. 19–38.
Solga, Heike (2012): Bildung und materielle Ungleichheit. Der investitve Sozialstaat auf dem Prüfstand. In: Becker, Rolf/Solga, Heike (eds.): Soziologische Bildungsforschung. Kölner Zeitschrift Für Soziologie und Sozialpsychologie, Sonderhefte, Vol. 52. Wiesbaden: Springer VS, pp. 459–487.
Solga, Heike (2014): Education, economic inequality and the promises of the social investment state. In: Socio-Economic Review, 12, pp. 269–297.
Stajić, Olivera/Gächter, August (2012): "Der falsche Teil der Wahrheit". In: Der Standard. 22-02-2012. https://www.derstandard.at/story/1329869977230/der-fal scheteil-der-wahrheit [Zugriff: 30.08.2023].
Statistics Austria (2021a): Frühe Schulabgänger und Schulabgängerinnen 1995 bis 2014. https://www.statistik.at/statistiken/bevoelkerung-und-soziales/bildung/bild ungsindikatoren [access: 22-12-2021].
Statistics Austria (2021b): Sozialausgaben im Corona-Jahr 2020 um 11% auf 130 Mrd. Euro gestiegen. Pressemitteilung 12.572-163/21.
Staub-Bernasconi, Silvia (2018): Soziale Arbeit als Handlungswissenschaft. Soziale Arbeit auf dem Weg zu kritischer Professionalität. UTB Soziale Arbeit. Opladen, Toronto: Verlag Barbara Budrich (UTB). 2nd ed.
Steiner, Mario/Pessl, Gabriele/Karaszek, Johannes (2015): Ausbildung bis 18. Grundlagenanalysen zum Bedarf von und Angebot für die Zielgruppe. Sozialpolitische Studienreihe, Vol. 20. Wien: ÖGB.
Steinert, Heinz/Pilgram, Arno (eds.) (2003): Welfare policy from Below. Struggles Against Social Exclusion in Europe. Aldershot: Ashgate.

Stelzer-Orthofer, Christine/Tamesberger, Dennis (2018): Die arbeitsmarktpolitische Agenda der schwarz-blauen Regierung: Symbolische Politik oder radikaler Umbau? In: WISO 41, 3, pp. 15–43.

Stelzer-Orthofer, Christine/Weidenholzer, Josef (eds.) (2011): Aktivierung und Mindestsicherung. Nationale und europäische Strategien gegen Armut und Arbeitslosigkeit. Mandelbaum: Wien.

Stemberger, Veronika/Katsivelaris, Niko/Zirkowitsch, Maximilian (2014): Soziale Arbeit in der Grundversorgung. Eine Skizze zur Bedeutung der organisierten Desintegration. In: soziales kapital, 12.

Stichweh, Rudolf (1997): Inklusion/Exklusion, funktionale Differenzierung und die Theorie der Weltgesellschaft. In: Soziale Systeme 3, pp. 123–136.

Sting, Stephan (2011): Jugend aus pädagogischer Sicht. In: BMWFJ (ed.): 6. Bericht zur Lage der Jugend in Österreich. Wien, pp. 39–42.

Sting, Stephan (2012): Zum Wandel der Jugendphase. Übergänge auf Dauer gestellt. In: Knapp, Gerald/Lauermann, Karin (eds.): Jugend, Gesellschaft und Soziale Arbeit. Klagenfurt, Ljubljana, Wien: Hermagoras, pp. 160–176.

Sting, Stephan (2015): Disziplin und Differenz. Soziale Arbeit in Österreich jenseits disziplinärer Identitätszwänge. In: soziales kapital, 14.

Sting, Stephan (2018): Bildung. In: Graßhoff, Gunther/Renker, Anna/Schröer, Wolfgang (eds.): Soziale Arbeit. Eine elementare Einführung. Lehrbuch. Wiesbaden, Heidelberg: Springer VS, pp. 399–411.

Sting, Stephan (2022): Selbstbildung. In: Kessl, Fabian/Reutlinger, Christian (eds.): Sozialraum. Eine elementare Einführung. Lehrbuch, Vol. 20. Wiesbaden, Heidelberg: Springer VS, pp. 243–252.

Sting, Stephan/Knecht, Alban (2022): Jugendzeit als Bildungszeit? Lebenslagenabhängige Veränderungen der Zeitlichkeit in jugendlichen Übergängen. In: Arlt, Florian/Heimgartner, Arno (eds.): Zeit und Offene Kinder- und Jugendarbeit. Soziale Arbeit/Social Issues. Wien, Münster: LIT, S. 57–76.

Straus, Florian (2012): Netzwerkarbeit: Förderung sozialer Ressourcen. In: Knecht, Alban/Schubert, Franz-Christian (eds.): Ressourcen im Sozialstaat und in der Sozialen Arbeit. Zuteilung – Förderung – Aktivierung. Stuttgart: Kohlhammer, pp. 224–237.

Stubbs, Paul/Lendvai-Bainton, Noémi (2020): Authoritarian Neoliberalism, Radical Conservatism and Social Policy within the European Union: Croatia, Hungary and Poland. In: Development and Change 51, 2, pp. 540–560.

Sußner, Petra (2018): Verfassungsblog: Gleich meint gleich! Warum sich Sozial-leistungen (auch) für Geflüchtete nicht ohne Weiteres kürzen lassen. https://verfassungsblog.de/gleich-meint-gleich-warum-sich-sozialleistungen-auch-fuer-gefluechtete-nicht-ohne-weiteres-kuerzen-lassen [access: 26-12-2022].

Swank, Duane/Betz, Hans-Georg (2019): Do Radical Right Populist Parties Matter? The Case of the European Welfare State. Presentation at the 2019 Annual Meetings of the APSA, August 29 – September 1, Washington DC.

Szigetvari, András (2018a): Regierung fixiert Ende der Lehre für Asylwerber. Laut dem Regierungssprecher ist ein eigener Aufenthaltstitel für Lehrlinge geplant. Die Rot-Weiß-Rot-Karte soll attraktiver werden. In: Der Standard, 26-08-2018 https://www.derstandard.at/story/2000086070416/fpoe-will-zugang-zur-lehre-fuer-asylwerbern-wieder-verbieten [access: 30-08-2023].

Szigetvari, András (2018b): Mehr Geld und Imagepolitur für die Lehre. In: Der Standard, 18-09-2018, S. 15.

Szigetvari, András (2020): Höchstgericht kippt Jobzugang für Asylwerber. In: Der Standard, 14-05-2020. https://www.derstandard.de/story/2000117496660/hoechstgericht-kippt-jobzugang-fuer-asylwerber [access: 30-08-2023].

Szigetvari, András (2021): Jobzugang für Asylwerber: Höchstgericht hebt Einschränkungen auf. In: Der Standard, 14-07-203. https://www.derstandard.at/story/2000128174346/jobzugang-fuer-asylwerber-hoechstgericht-hebt-einschraenkungen-auf [access: 30-08-2023].

Tálos, Emmerich (2004): Umbau des Sozialstaates? Österreich und Deutschland im Vergleich. In: Politische Vierteljahresschrift 45, 2, pp. 213–236.

Tálos, Emmerich (2006): Sozialpolitik. Zwischen Expansion und Restriktion. In: Dachs, Herbert/Gerlich, Peter/Gottweis, Herbert/Kramer, Helmut/Lauber, Volkmar/Müller, Wolfgang C. (eds.): Politik in Österreich. Das Handbuch. Wien: Manz, 624-636.

Tálos, Emmerich/Obinger, Herbert (2019): Schwarz-blaue Sozialpolitik. Der österreichische Sozialstaat unter Druck. In: Tálos, Emmerich (ed.): Die schwarz-blaue Wende in Österreich. Eine Bilanz. Wien: LIT-Verlag, pp. 231–257.

Täubig, Vicki (2009): Totale Institution Asyl. Empirische Befunde zu alltäglichen Lebensführungen in der organisierten Desintegration. Weinheim: Juventa.

Therborn, Göran (2013): The Killing Fields of Inequality. Cambridge, UK, Malden, MA, USA: polity.

Theurl, Simon (2022): Wie exzessives Sanktionieren von Arbeitslosen den Versicherungsschutz untergräbt. Wien.

Thiersch, Hans (2014): Lebensweltorientierte Soziale Arbeit. Aufgaben der Praxis im sozialen Wandel. Edition soziale Arbeit. Weinheim: Beltz. 9th ed.

Thiersch, Hans/Grunwald, Klaus/Köngeter, S. (2012): Lebensweltorientierte Soziale Arbeit. In: Thole, Werner (ed.): Grundriss Soziale Arbeit. Ein einführendes Handbuch. Wiesbaden: VS. 4th ed., pp. 175–196.

Törnblom, Kjell/Kazemi, Ali (eds.) (2012): Handbook of Social Resource Theory. Theoretical Extensions, Empirical Insights, and Social Applications. Berlin, Heidelberg, New York: Springer.

Uske, Hans (1995): Das Fest der Faulenzer. Duisburg: DISS.

Uske, Hans (2000): "Sozialschmarotzer" und "Versager". Missachtung und Anerkennung in Diskursen über Massenarbeitslosigkeit. In: Holtgrewe, Ursula/Vosswinkel, Stephan/Wagner, Gabriele (eds.): Anerkennung und Arbeit. Analyse und Forschung Sozialwissenschaften. Konstanz: UVK, pp. 169–192.

Verein Wiener Jugendzentren (2008): Partizipation. Zur Theorie und Praxis politischer Bildung in der Jugendarbeit. Wien: Verein Wiener Jugendzentren im Eigenverlag.

Verfassungsgerichtshof (2019): Sozialhilfe-Grundsatzgesetz: Höchstsatzsystem für Kinder und Arbeitsqualifizierungsbonus verfassungswidrig. Mitteilung, 17-12-2019 zum VfGH-Erkenntnis vom 12-12-2019. Wien.

Verfassungsgerichtshof (2021): Erlässe zu Beschäftigungsbewilligungen für Asylwerbende sind gesetzwidrig. Mitteilung vom 14.7.2021 zu VfGH-Erkenntnis V 95-96/2021, 23-06-2021. Wien.

Wacker, Konstantin (2007): Teure neue Lehrstelle. Eine Untersuchung zur Effizienz des Blum-Bonus. Wien.

Wacquant, Loïc (2009): Punishing the Poor: The Neoliberal Government of Social Insecurity. Durham (North Carolina): Duke University Press.
Wagner, Heinz (2020): Lager Traiskirchen ist kein Ort für Kinderflüchtlinge. In: Kurier, 21.11.2020. https://kurier.at/kiku/lager-traiskirchen-ist-kein-ort-fuer-kinderfluechtlinge/401104944 [access: 30-08-2023].
Wagner, Thomas (2014): Die Mitmachfalle. Bürgerbeteiligung als Herrschaftsinstrument. Köln: PapyRossa. 2nd ed.
Walker, Melanie (2005): Amartya Sen's Capability Approach and Education. In: Educational Action Research 13, 1, pp. 103–110.
Walther, Andreas (2006): Von der Jugendberufshilfe zu einer Sozialpädagogik des Übergangs? In: Schweppe, Cornelia/Sting, Stephan (eds.): Sozialpädagogik im Übergang. Neue Herausforderungen für Disziplin, Profession und Ausbildung. Weinheim, München: Juventa, pp. 205–220.
Walther, Andreas (2012): Schwierige Jugendliche – prekäre Übergänge? Ein biografischer und international vergleichender Blick auf Herausforderungen im Übergang vom Jugend- in das Erwachsenenalter. In: Thielen, Marc/Katzenbach, Dieter/Schnell, Irmtraud (eds.): Prekäre Übergänge? Erwachsenwerden unter den Bedingungen von Behinderung und Benachteiligung. Bad Heilbrunn: Julius Klinkhardt, pp. 13–35.
Walther, Andreas (2015): Bildung und Bewältigung in unterschiedlichen Lebenslaufregimen. Ein Beitrag zu einer international vergleichenden sozialpädagogischen Forschung. In: Parreira do Amaral, Marcelo/Amos, Sigrid Karin (eds.): Internationale und vergleichende Erziehungswissenschaft. Geschichte, Theorie, Methode und Forschungsfelder. New frontiers in comparative education, Vol. 2. Münster: Waxmann, pp. 189–208.
Walther, Andreas (2019): Teilhabe als Partizipation – und als Problem? Praktiken der Beteiligung Jugendlicher zwischen Adressierung, Aneignung und Anerkennung. In: Sozialpädagogik, Kommission (ed.): Teilhabe durch*in*trotz Sozialpädagogik. Veröffentlichungen der Kommission Sozialpädagogik. Weinheim: Beltz Juventa.
Walther, Andreas/Walter, Sibylle/Pohl, Axel (2007): "Du wirst echt in eine Schublade gesteckt." Junge Frauen und Männer im Übergangssystem zwischen Wahlbiographie und Cooling-Out. In: Stauber, Barbara/Pohl, Axel/Walther, Andreas (eds.): Subjektorientierte Übergangsforschung. Weinheim: Juventa, pp. 97–129.
Walzer, M. (1998): Sphären der Gerechtigkeit. Frankfurt/M.: Fischer.
Wellgraf, Stefan (2014): Hauptschüler. Zur gesellschaftlichen Produktion von Verachtung. Kultur und soziale Praxis. Bielefeld: transcript.
Wellgraf, Stefan (2018): Schule der Gefühle. Zur emotionalen Erfahrung von Minderwertigkeit in neoliberalen Zeiten. Bielefeld: transcript.
Wendt, Wolf Rainer (2010): Das ökosoziale Prinzip. Soziale Arbeit ökologisch verstanden. Freiburg: Lambertus.
Werner, Emmy E. (1977): Kauai's children come of age. Honolulu: University Press of Hawaii.
Wiezorek, Christine/Pardo-Puhlmann, Margaret (2013): Armut, Bildungsferne, Erziehungsunfähigkeit. In: Dietrich, Fabian/Heinrich, Martin/Thieme, Nina (eds.): Bildungsgerechtigkeit jenseits von Chancengleichheit. Wiesbaden: Springer VS, pp. 197–214.
WKO (2022a): Bildungsförderung in Österreich. Förderung der betrieblichen Ausbildung von Lehrlingen – Mädchen in "Männerberufen". Wien.

WKO (2022b): Förderungen für Lehrbetriebe. Förderarten im Überblick. Wien.
Wodak, Ruth (ed.) (2007): Methods of critical discourse analysis. Introducing qualitative methods. London: SAGE. Reprinted.
Wodak, Ruth (2020): Politik mit der Angst. Wien, Hamburg: Edition Konturen. 2nd ed.
Wogawa, Diane (2000): Missbrauch im Sozialstaat. Eine Analyse des Missbrauchsarguments im politischen Diskurs. Wiesbaden: Westdeutscher Verlag.
Woltran, Iris (2018): EuGH kippt gekürzte Mindestsicherung für Menschen mit "Asyl auf Zeit", 28-11-2018. A&W Blog. Wien.
Wyss, Kurt (2010): Workfare – Praktische Ideologie gegen Erwerbslose und Armutsbetroffene. In: Schulhefte, 138, pp. 76–85.
Yanow, Dvora (1992): Silence in public disourse: Organisational and policy myths. In: Journal of Public Adminstration Research and Theory 2, 4, pp. 399–423.
Zandonella, Martina (2020): Ökonomische Ungleichheit zerstört die Demokratie. Wenn Armutsbetroffene nicht zu Wahlen gehen und ihre Anliegen kein Gehör finden. In: Appel, Margit/Fabris, Verena/Knecht, Alban et al. (eds.): Stimmen gegen Armut. Weil soziale Ungleichheit und Ausgrenzung die Demokratie gefährden. Norderstedt: BoD-Verlag, pp. 83–93.
ZARA (2000–2010): ZARA-Rassismusreporte 2000–2020.
Zaunbauer, Wolfgang (2019): Jugendvertrauensräte werden nicht abgeschafft. Im Regierungsprogramm war die Abschaffung des Lehrlings-Betriebsrats vorgesehen. Nun verzichtet die Koalition darauf. In: Kurier.
Ziegler, Holger (2009): Zum Stand der Wirtschaftsforschung in der Sozialen Arbeit. In: Jugendhilfe 47, 3, pp. 180–187.
Ziegler, Holger (2011): Gerechtigkeit und Soziale Arbeit: Capabilities als Antwort auf das Maßstabsproblem in der Sozialen Arbeit. In: Böllert, Karin (ed.): Soziale Arbeit als Wohlfahrtsproduktion. Wiesbaden: VS, pp. 153–166.
Zimmermann, Michaela (2010): Jugendbeteiligung in Österreich. In: Gaiser, Wolfgang/Lindner, Lisa (eds.): Partizipation junger Menschen. Nationale Perspektiven und europäischer Kontext. special, Vol. 6. Bonn: Jugend für Europa, pp. 194–199.

10 Index

accumulation 24, 80
activating measures 37, 42, 51, 55, 72, 81
activating social policy 37, 87, 104
activating welfare state 34, 86
activation 14, 16, 17, 33, 38, 52, 59, 71, 84, 85, 96, 97, 98
AMS 11, 48, 58, 59, 62, 63, 65, 67, 68, 81, 92, 104, 106
anti-elitism 40
anti-establishment 40
apprenticeship 15, 51, 53, 57, 58, 59, 61, 62
   compensation 66
   in-company 61, 62, 66
   positions 51, 58, 59, 61, 62, 65, 96, 97, 106
   qualification 61
   shortage occupation 63, 64, 67, 68, 79
apprenticeship allowance 58
apprenticeship subsidies 58, 60, 66, 72
asylum-seeking youth 60, 63, 64, 67, 78, 87, 98
Ausbildungsfit 61, 83, 104, 106
Austrian Federal Youth Representation (Österreichische Bundesjugendvertretung) 92
authoritarianism 40
Bartenstein Decree 60, 63
Black-Blue Coalition (of ÖVP and FPÖ) 19, 72, 73, 78, 86
Blair-Schroeder-Paper 36
BZÖ 19
capabilities 28
capability approach (CA) 21, 26, 28, 34, 35, 38, 39
child and youth work 54
childcare 36
co-determination 39, 75, 91, 93
compulsory education 55

compulsory kindergarten year 72
compulsory schooling 64, 97
compulsory training 45, 51, 52, 64, 68, 75, 85, 97
content-analytical evaluation 18
co-production 80, 90, 95
counselling 30, 31, 54, 84, 88, 98
critical discourse analysis 19
day care centres 14
democracy 39, 42, 93, 99
disciplining 14, 16, 17, 41, 84
discourse 14, 32, 44
   administrative-political 44
   distribution-relevant 32
   institutional 44
discourse analysis 20, 34, 43
discrimination 53, 55
document analysis 18, 19
double mandate 16
early promoting state 37
early school leaver 12
economisation 15, 17
education 25, 33
educational policies 13
educational resources 14, 42, 72, 73
emancipation 16, 54, 55, 81, 93, 96
employability 33, 42, 94, 95
empowerment 93
entrepreneurial self 38
EU Youth Strategy 91
everyday life 29
exclusionary policies 41, 68, 77
expert interviewing 18
external resources 90
flexibilization 37
fordern und fördern 17, 38
Fordist-Keynesian model 13
FPÖ (Freedom Party of Austria) 19, 65
guiding principles 29, 33, 34, 37, 38, 71, 96
Hartz IV 14, 15, 35

137

health 18, 21, 22, 23, 24, 25, 26, 28, 29, 38, 50, 59, 72, 74, 109
help and control 17
human capital 14
identity process 16
incentive mechanisms 35, 65, 71, 72, 80, 95
inequality 22, 24, 26, 28, 31, 33, 37, 70, 75
inequality structure 39
inequality theory 22
informational basis of the judgement of justice (IBJJ) 38, 70
institutional analysis 20
Integration Year Act 68
interdisciplinarity 21
International Federation of Social Workers 96
interpretive policy analysis 18, 43
Keynesian social policy 34
labour market 12, 13, 18, 51
labour market integration 64, 86
labour market policy 17
legitimation 37, 55
marginalisation 55
material resources 23, 35, 42, 54, 73
means-tested minimum income scheme 19
meritocracy 75
mission models 33
monetary resources 26, 38, 42, 49, 66, 72, 98
motivation 55, 90
multidimensionality 21, 22, 42
multi-level approach 28, 32
National Council 19
nationalism 40
nativism 40
neoliberalism 13, 16, 33, 34, 35, 42
neo-social 35
open youth work 16, 52, 61, 83, 91, 93
ÖVP (Austrian People's Party) 19, 46, 57, 65, 96
parasites 45

participation 24, 34, 37, 39, 40, 53, 58, 64, 71, 80, 81, 83, 87, 91, 92, 95, 98, 99
policy analysis 34
policy field analysis 18
political discourse 36
post-war period 13
poverty 31, 37, 41, 48, 49, 53, 54, 70, 75
   multidimensional 22
poverty policy 77
precarisation 37
precarity 75
professionals 31, 92
pronatalism 40
psychological resource theories 23
psychological/mental resources 23, 31, 36, 42, 51, 64, 70, 73, 90, 95
psychotherapy 71
public discourse 36, 45, 75, 77
punishment 17
punitivity 14, 17, 40, 41, 46, 84, 85, 96, 97
quasi-pedagogical function of markets 36
Red-Black Coalition (of SPÖ and ÖVP) 19, 63, 64, 71, 74, 78, 86, 98
Red-White-Red Card 68, 79, 80
renationalisation 40
resilience theory 23
resource dependence theory 32
resource endowment 22
resource exchange theory 23
Resource Theory (IMTM) 18, 21, 23, 25, 30, 32, 37
resource theory of social inequality and social policy 22
resource-oriented action 90
resource-oriented social work 31
responsibilisation 14, 16
right-wing populism 40
right-wing populist/extreme right social policy 71
right-wing populist/extreme right social policy model 39, 40

salutogenesis model 23
sanctions 16
school 25
school social work 71
scrounger 45
self-control 16
self-efficacy 11, 31, 54, 55, 70, 88, 90, 93
self-responsibility 16, 38
shirkers 45
social coping 24
social inequality 14, 21, 23, 24, 25, 95
social investment 15, 33, 36, 42, 46
social investment approach 14, 34, 75
social investment state 14, 86
social pedagogy 16, 38, 54, 88, 91, 96
social policy 14, 18, 34, 40
social work 15, 16, 31, 38, 52, 88, 91, 96
sociological theory of inequality 21
spectrum of resources 18, 26, 31, 95, 98
SPÖ (Austrian Social Democratic Party) 19, 46, 57, 60, 61, 96
street-level bureaucracy 33, 44, 90
Supra-Company Training (SCT) 53, 61, 65, 66, 69, 72, 83, 92, 104, 106
theory of resource conservation 23
theory of social inequality 21, 22, 24
training guarantee 15, 45, 62, 63, 75

training obligation (Ausbildung bis 18) 15, 45, 46, 61, 62
Training up to 18 46, 53, 62, 64, 74, 85
transactional resource concept 30
transformation 13, 22
transition 11
triple mandate 31
types of capital (Bourdieu) 23, 24, 26
Tyrol 65
unemployment 12, 37, 44, 45, 48, 58, 62, 68, 71, 74, 83, 86, 99, 102, 104
unemployment assistance 15
unemployment benefits 15
unemployment rates 12
Vienna 14, 65, 91, 92
vocational education and training 11, 15
Vocational Youth Welfare (Jugendberufshilfe) 15, 18
Vorarlberg 65
welfare regimes 35
welfare state 13, 14, 40, 81
welfare state 'from below' 81
women-at-the-stove policy 41
work-first policy 15
Youth Coaching 50, 51, 52, 54, 61, 62, 83, 84, 89, 93, 97, 104, 106
Youth Confidence Councils (Jugendvertrauensräte) 75, 91
youth councils 91
youth parliaments 91

Elina Fonsén | Raisa Ahtiainen
Marja Heikkinen | Lauri Heikonen
Petra Strehmel | Emanuel Tamir (eds.)

Early Childhood Education Leadership in Times of Crisis

International Studies During the COVID-19

2023 • 264 pp. • Paperback • 39,90 € (D) • 41,10 € (A)
ISBN 978-3-8474-2683-7 • also available as e-book in open access

The COVID-19 pandemic has dramatically affected all aspects of professional and private life worldwide, including the field of early childhood education and care (ECE). This volume sheds light on leadership in ECE: How did leaders experience the challenges they were facing and what coping strategies did they apply in order to deal with the changes in everyday life and practices in ECE centres? Authors from twelve countries present empirical findings gaining information on different crisis management mechanisms in ECE systems around the world.

www.shop.budrich.de

Printed in the USA
CPSIA information can be obtained
at www.ICGtesting.com
JSHW011542040324
58548JS00017B/387